SIN PATRÓN

SINFATRON

SIN PATRÓN

Stories from Argentina's
Worker-Run Factories

the lavaca collective

Translated by Katherine Kohlstedt
in cooperation with Federico Moreno,
Julian Massaldi-Fuchs, Avi Lewis, and Lance Selfa

Haymarket Books
Chicago, Illinois

First published in 2004 by lavaca in Buenos Aires, Argentina
© 2004 lavaca collective
Translation © 2007 Haymarket Books

Published in 2007 by Haymarket Books
PO Box 180165, Chicago, IL 60618
773-583-7884
www.haymarketbooks.org

Cover design by Amy Balkin
Cover photograph of workers at the recovered factory, Forja, in San Martin,
Buenos Aires, after a showing of the film, The Take.
Photo courtesy of Andres D'Elia.

ISBN-13: 978-1931859-43-1

Trade distribution:
In the U.S. through Consortium Book Sales, www.cbsd.com
In the UK, Turnaround Publisher Services, www.turnaround-psl.com
In Australia, Palgrave MacMillan, www.palgravemacmillan.com.au

This book was published with the generous support of the Wallace Global Fund

Printed in Canada by union labor on recycled paper containing 50 percent post-
consumer waste in accordance with the guidelines of the Green Press Initiative,
www.greenpressinitiative.org

10 9 8 7 6 5 4 3 2

Contents

Foreword

Naomi Klein and Avi Lewis

On March 19, 2003, we were on the roof of the Zanón ceramic tile factory, filming an interview with Cepillo. He was showing us how the workers fended off eviction by armed police, defending their democratic workplace with slingshots and the little ceramic balls normally used to pound the Patagonian clay into raw material for tiles. His aim was impressive. It was the day the bombs started falling on Baghdad.

As journalists, we had to ask ourselves what we were doing there. What possible relevance could there be in this one factory at the southernmost tip of our continent, with its band of radical workers and its David and Goliath narrative, when bunker-busting apocalypse was descending on Iraq?

But we, like so many others, had been drawn to Argentina to witness firsthand an explosion of activism in the wake of its 2001 crisis—a host of dynamic new social movements that were not only advancing a bitter critique of the economic model that had destroyed their country, but were busily building local alternatives in the rubble.

There were many popular responses to the crisis, from neighborhood assemblies and barter clubs, to resurgent left-wing parties and mass movements of the unemployed, but we spent most of our year in Argentina with workers in "recovered companies." Almost entirely under the media radar, workers in Argentina have been responding to rampant unemployment and capital flight by taking over traditional businesses that have gone bankrupt and are reopening them under democratic worker management. It's an old idea reclaimed and retrofitted for a brutal new time. The principles are so simple, so elementally fair, that they seem more self-evident than radical when articulated by one of the workers in this book: "We formed the cooperative with the criteria of equal wages and making basic decisions by assembly; we are against the separation of manual and intellectual work; we want a rotation of positions and; above all, the ability to recall our elected leaders."

The movement of recovered companies is not epic in scale—some 170 companies, around 10,000 workers in Argentina. But six years on, and unlike some of the country's other new movements, it has survived and continues to build quiet strength in the midst of the country's deeply unequal "recovery." Its tenacity is a function of its pragmatism: this is a movement that is based on action, not talk. And its defining action, reawakening the means of production under worker control, while loaded with potent symbolism, is anything but symbolic. It is feeding families, rebuilding shattered pride, and opening a window of powerful possibility.

Like a number of other emerging social movements around the world, the workers in the recovered companies are rewriting the traditional script for how change is supposed to happen.

Rather than following anyone's ten-point plan for revolution, the workers are darting ahead of the theory—at least, straight to the part where they get their jobs back. In Argentina, the theorists are chasing after the factory workers, trying to analyze what is already in noisy production.

These struggles have had a tremendous impact on the imaginations of activists around the world. At this point there are many more starry-eyed grad papers on the phenomenon than there are recovered companies. But there is also a renewed interest in democratic workplaces from Durban to Melbourne to New Orleans.

That said, the movement in Argentina is as much a product of the globalization of alternatives as it is one of its most contagious stories. Argentine workers borrowed the slogan, "Occupy, Resist, Produce" from Latin America's largest social movement, Brazil's Movimiento Sin Terra, in which more than a million people have reclaimed unused land and put it back into community production. One worker told us that what the movement in Argentina is doing is "MST for the cities." In South Africa, we saw a protester's T-shirt with an even more succinct summary of this new impatience: Stop Asking, Start Taking.

But as much as these similar sentiments are blossoming in different parts of the world for the same reasons, there is an urgent need to share these stories and tools of resistance even more widely. For that reason, this translation that you are holding is of tremendous importance: it's the first comprehensive portrait of Argentina's famous movement of recovered companies in English.

The book's author is the lavaca collective, itself a worker cooperative like the struggles documented here. While we were in Argentina filming our documentary, *The Take*, we ran into lavaca members wherever the workers' struggles led—the courts, the legislature, the streets, the factory floor. They do some of the most sophisticated engaged journalism in the world today.

And this book is classic lavaca. That means it starts with a montage—a theoretical framework that is unabashedly poetic. Then it cuts to a fight scene of the hard facts: the names, the numbers, and the m.o. behind the armed robbery that was Argentina's crisis. With the scene set, the book then zooms in to the stories of individual struggles, told almost entirely through the testimony of the workers themselves.

This approach is deeply respectful of the voices of the protagonists, while still leaving plenty of room for the authors' observations, at once playful and scathing. In this interplay between the cooperatives that inhabit the book and the one that produced it, there are a number of themes that bear mention.

First of all, there is the question of ideology. This movement is frustrating to some on the Left who feel it is not clearly anticapitalist, those who chafe at how comfortably it exists within the market economy and see worker management as merely a new form of auto-exploitation. Others see the project of cooperativism, the legal form chosen by the vast majority of the recovered companies, as a capitulation in itself—insisting that only full nationalization by the state can bring worker democracy into a broader socialist project.

In the words of the workers, and between the lines, you get a sense of these tensions and the complex relationship between various struggles and parties of the Left in Argentina. Workers in the movement are generally suspicious of being co-opted to anyone's political agenda, but at the same time cannot afford to turn down any support. More interesting by far is to see how workers in this movement are politicized *by* the struggle, which begins with the most basic imperative: workers want to work, to feed their families. You can see in this book how some of the most powerful new working-class leaders in Argentina today discovered solidarity on a path that started from that essentially apolitical point.

Whether you think the movement's lack of a leading ideology is a tragic weakness or a refreshing strength, this book makes clear precisely how the recovered companies challenge capitalism's most cherished ideal: the sanctity of private property.

The legal and political case for worker control in Argentina does not only rest on the unpaid wages, evaporated benefits, and emptied-out pension funds. The workers make a sophisticated case for their moral right to property—in this case, the machines and physical premises—based not just on what they're owed personally, but what society is owed. The recovered companies propose themselves as an explicit remedy to all the corporate welfare, corruption, and other forms of public subsidy the owners enjoyed in the process of bankrupting their firms and moving their wealth to safety, abandoning whole communities to the twilight of economic exclusion.

This argument is, of course, available for immediate use in the United States. But this story goes much deeper than corporate welfare, and that's where the Argentine experience will really resonate with North Americans. It's become axiomatic on the left to say that Argentina's crash was a direct result of the IMF orthodoxy imposed on the country with such enthusiasm in the neoliberal 1990s. What this book makes clear is that in Argentina, just as in the U.S. occupation of Iraq, those bromides about private sector efficiency were nothing more than a cover story for an explosion of frontier-style plunder—looting on a massive scale by a small group of elites. Privatization, deregulation, labor flexibility: these were the tools to facilitate a massive transfer of public wealth to private hands, not to mention private debts to the public purse. Like Enron traders, the businessmen who haunt the pages of this book learned the first lesson of capitalism and stopped there: greed is good, and more greed is better. As one worker says in the book, "There are guys that wake up in the morning thinking about how to screw people, and others who think, how do we rebuild this Argentina that they have torn apart?"

In the answer to that question, you can read a powerful story of transformation. This book takes as a key premise that capitalism produces and distributes not just goods and services, but identities. When the capital and its carpetbaggers had flown, what was left was not only companies that had been emptied, but a whole hollowed-out country filled with people whose identities—as workers—had been stripped away too.

As one of the organizers in the movement wrote to us, "It is a huge amount of work to recover a company. But the real work is to recover a worker and that is the task that we have just begun."

On April 17, 2003, we were on Avenida Jujuy in Buenos Aires, standing with the Brukman workers and a huge crowd of their supporters in front of a fence, behind which was a small army of police guarding the Brukman factory. After a brutal eviction, the workers were determined to get back to work at their sewing machines.

In Washington, D.C. that day, USAID announced that it had chosen Bechtel Corporation as the prime contractor for the reconstruction of Iraq's architecture. The heist was about to begin in earnest, both in the United States and in Iraq. Deliberately induced crisis was providing the cover for the transfer of billions of tax dollars to a handful of politically connected corporations.

In Argentina, they'd already seen this movie—the wholesale plunder of public wealth, the explosion of unemployment, the shredding of the social fabric, the staggering human consequences. And fifty-two seamstresses were in the street, backed by thousands of others, trying to take back what was already theirs. It was definitely the place to be.

Avi Lewis and Naomi Klein
March 2007

Workers of Another Class

In ages favorable to imposters, it's prime time for business interests to masquerade as public opinion. Lobbyists honk their own horns in hopes of blocking news traffic, and what manages to get through follows the mathematical rule of exclusion: there is more left out of the media agenda than in it. And the little that remains is disfigured.

That is how these times are presented—perverse and cruel.

And the media we have to help us interpret them is really a pill that causes impotence.

Whatever we look at, it all looks wrong.

And, blindfolded by the horror of all this, we are left with neither the energy nor the patience to believe in anything.

◆ ◆ ◆

Nomen est numen.

To name is to know.

To revive this old maxim is not simply to say the names out

loud, but also the concepts, viewpoints, and stories that weave together a complex and diverse reality.

It is not about simplifying it.

It is not about pointing your finger at what is good or what is
bad, or even about distinguishing the real from the ephemeral.

It is about naming everything, even what seems pointless.

Because this is the only power of information—converting
deeds into words.

◆ ◆ ◆

This is a story of change.

But since, like all sins, it leaves us with a penance instead of a
lesson, we'll avoid prognoses.

The limit of all predictions is what people are capable of
doing.

It is not chance, but courage, that makes the future unpre-
dictable.

That is what this story and this change are about.

◆ ◆ ◆

To create change is to transform a paradigm. It's a process in
which intensity depends not on quantity, but on perseverance.
One drop at a time.

If we begin by understanding capitalism not so much as a system that produces and distributes goods, but more as a producer
and distributor of identities, then each change is marked by a
transformation of the paradigms that determine the perspectives of
these identities. But how do we detect them?

Adam Smith identified one: the wealth of a nation depends

exclusively on the skill of its labor and the proportion[1] of productive to unproductive workers. Marx pointed out the definitive factor—the ownership of the means of production.

For Smith and Marx, a society's mode of production forms the axis of the theory.

Today thier theories are historic accounts that allow us to reconstruct the groundwork of industrial capitalism. However, the changes they registered weren't evident until they occurred. That is to say, the first thing we can learn from the old teachers is that there is no guarantee that new ideas, values, or processes will be genuinely decisive in social history.[2]

Until they are.

♦   ♦   ♦

The classic division of the economy determined, until recently, the existence of three sectors: primary (agriculture and livestock), secondary (industry), and tertiary (services). This division produced, according to the level of development of each sector, a corresponding social pyramid, with its different classes and identities. The whole formed a single economic body and a single social organization: the nation-state.

Global capitalism broke these molds, and, with them, the political and cultural implications derived from that structure.

It drove a stake through the heart of the local bourgeoisies, quartered the division of labor, scattering the pieces to every corner of the globe and, in doing this, killed all theoretical systems that support and oppose industrial capitalism.

As Zygmunt Bauman describes, "Henry Ford depended on

his workers for his wealth and power as much as the workers depended on him and his aides for their livelihood.... Both sides knew that they would meet again—the next day, and in the months and years to come. This time perspective allowed them to perceive their relations as a 'conflict of interest.'"[3] Those were the days of "solid capitalism," according to Bauman's definition, where the nation-state represented the principal stage upon which those struggles would be played out.

Toward the end of the twentieth century the scene got complicated, like in those video games where each level imposes bigger challenges. "By the end of the twentieth century the normative powers of nation-states, and particularly their practical capacity for sovereign normative regulation, have been thoroughly eroded. Business (and particularly big business, the business that truly counts when it comes to the balancing of state books and securing the livelihood of state subjects) has made a successful bid or secession from the realm of sovereignty. The economic foundations of human survival and well-being are now once more politically 'extraterritorial,' just as they used to be two centuries ago, at the threshold of the modern era, when business managed to escape from the tight ethical supervision of the local community into a 'no man's land' not yet occupied and administered by the emergent modern state—into a veritable frontier-land where the 'cash nexus' was the sole social bond and cut-throat competition the sole law of the country."[4]

As Uruguayan writer Raúl Zibechi sums it up, "Capitalism's reason to exist is accumulation, a process that ends up producing surpluses of capital and labor. These surpluses hinder or obstruct the continuity of the accumulation process. This can only be resolved by the destruction or degradation of production and the transfer of capital to other areas or regions to avoid its devaluation.... None of this is new. However, as David Harvey points out in *The New Imperialism*, the previous capitalist equilibrium has been broken, giving way to the old modes of accumulation. They reappear in new forms, which he calls 'accumulation by dispossession.'[5] They are similar to what Marx called 'primitive accumulation of capital,' which were never abandoned by the bourgeoisie, but appear to be a hallmark of capitalism in its period of decadence."[6]

This is what Bauman calls liquid modernity, which means nothing less than a return to the most brutal and primitive production conditions.

◆ ◆ ◆

According to the theoretical systems that analyzed industrial capitalism, labor determined one's social class, but it also determined the potential for change and the caliber of each conflict, among other things.

Globalization destroyed the interaction of these forces, reducing them to what they essentially were—mere relationships of exploitation.

In the first place, to focus on what interests us for this story, wage labor has turned into "flexible labor" or "trash jobs,"[7] thus creating a new social category—a non-class. There are no rights, or the possibility of winning them, when all that matters, day after day, is securing mere subsistence.

The extinction of the traditional industrial proletariat in a nutshell was written, word for word, by Pierre Bourdieu and a team of sociologists. He called it *The Misery of the World* and, in his effort to record the "profound disintegration of the industrial order and, consequently, the social order," he interviewed those soon to become relics in the social museum. It is an account of "all the distance that separates the proletariat—although weakened or in decay, with lower but regular wages, bank accounts in order, and a relatively secure future—and the worker whose descent into unemployment, with no protection or guarantees, leaves him in a sub-proletarian condition: abandoned, unorganized, obsessed with surviving, hanging by his fingernails, day to day, between unpaid rents and unpayable debts."[8]

Unemployment—that is to say, *the absence of work*—therefore became not only a new social category, but also an alternative.

The land of exclusion from the labor market and, therefore, from class identities, is so broad, deep, and vast that it becomes a whole other world.

A parallel universe that needs to create, out of nothing, everything that it is denied.

◆　◆　◆

Harvey Brooks defined technology as "the use of scientific knowledge to specify ways of doing things in a *reproducible* manner."[9] Applying his point of view, unemployed workers have created a social technology that we attempt to name here, without prioritizing its components, but, instead, looking at the whole formula.

It is the direct consequence of what Daniel Bell titled *The Disintegration of Capitalism* in 1955, and whose rotting corpse was left exposed in Argentina near the end of 2001.

Bell's argument was the following:

First, capitalism had to be understood not only as an economic system, but as a social system, linked through the company, which provided the system's social glue and, at the same time, a community and a continuity of interests. Then came the fragmentation of family-owned capitalism—in part due to the banks and investment funds—the most important result being the mutation of the ruling class—from the national bourgeoisie to the corporate managers and CEOs. This meant, among other things, that power would no longer be in the hands of a specific social group, with its corresponding interests, adversaries, and conflicts, but within a technical class, whose members would pass through the revolving door from a corporation's board of directors to the top levels of government agencies.

Finally, the consequences. Bell says that there are silent revolutions taking place in the relationship between power and social class.

◆　◆　◆

For Bell, these revolutions include a change that he noted in an article published in *Fortune,* where he analyzed the global composition of labor. It was the 1950s and Naomi Klein had not even been born yet, but the brilliant theory about the change in capitalist production that she would develop in her book *No Logo* had already found powerful strands of DNA in Bell's work. Capitalism increasingly cared less about producing objects and concentrated on turning the formula around—instead, the creation of culture (understood as the distribution of identities), the control of political power structures, and the outsourcing of heavy tasks, such as economic production. A parody of Bill Clinton's famous phrase,

"It's the economy, stupid."

Ralf Dahrendorf had also pointed out that what counts in industrial society is authority, not property, and that, with the disappearance of the owner, a separation occurs between the political and economic orders. That class position no longer determines the positions of authority in the political class.[10]

The unfortunate Bell labeled his theory *the postindustrial society*. "In Western society we are in the midst of a vast historical change in which old social relations (which were property-bound), existing power structures (centered on narrow elites), and bourgeois culture (based on notions of restraint and delayed gratification) are being rapidly eroded.... What these new social forms will be like is not completely clear. Nor is it likely that they will achieve the unity of the economic system and character structure which was characteristic of capitalist civilization from the mid-eighteenth to the mid-twentieth century. The use of the hyphenated prefix *post-* indicates, thus, that sense of living in interstitial time."[11]

In fact, smitten by his predictions about the role technology and knowledge were to play in the future, Bell had actually taken a step backward. He was describing something that had already been named—the disintegration of a system.

This story is about what happened to the crumbs left over.

◆ ◆ ◆

Industrial capitalism didn't die of natural causes. Even less so in Latin America.

In the first place, because, "according to all the analyses at our disposal, even from varying perspectives, the welfare state was an institution that enabled the regulation of the mass production society, characterized by the Taylorist division of labor, the Ford assembly line, and the central role of the specialized worker. It was the rebellion of the workers and popular sectors of the Third World that demolished the whole framework built after the crisis of 1929."[12]

Second, because these rebellions planted the seeds for important waves of victories followed by absolute losses of rights. Without any gray area, Argentina went straight from being a country with model labor legislation to a model of flexible labor and unprecedented unemployment.

The turning point between one and the other was the military dictatorship.

Writer Rodolfo Walsh was the first to condemn it in the open letter he wrote days before being kidnapped and disappeared by the Argentine military. In that letter he denounced torture, kidnappings, and killings on the first anniversary of the coup, also writing that, "it is in this government's economic policy where we will find not just the explanation for its crimes, but also a greater atrocity that punishes millions of human beings with planned misery."[13]

◆ ◆ ◆

Planned misery.

What was Walsh referring to?

Let's see: massive wage cuts, income redistribution and a brutal concentration of wealth, record unemployment, the collapse of consumption, an exodus of professionals due to the "rationalization" or "flexibilization" of the economy, historic external debt, the atrophy of the welfare state, blind obedience to IMF nostrums, and the reign of the monopolies and what was called the "new speculative oligarchy."

There's more: privatization of banks, foreign control over internal savings and credit, rewards for companies that defraud the state.

For Walsh, the military's greatest crime was not the daily atrocities, but the economic plan that was, in many ways, a premonition of the practice called neoliberalism—an absolute, timeless, and metaphysical market.

Argentina opened its economy indiscriminately, began the destruction of its industry, and inaugurated what was known as the "Hood Robin State." Robin Hood reversed, taking from the poor to give to the rich, as the statistics on growing economic inequality continue to show.

◆ ◆ ◆

The military dictatorship fell in the wake of the madness of the Falklands (Malvinas) War. The new weak democracy was born into a society that hadn't taken it back in the streets, but was handed it thanks to the ineptitude of the military.

Raúl Alfonsín's government (1983–1989) was a dubious mix of victim and accomplice of this economy concentrated in such few hands. Since he didn't finish the job, then came Carlos Menem to round out the dirty work. Menem finished the plan that Walsh had condemned in his letter, correcting and amplifying it under "democracy" between 1989 and 1999. Argentina had entered the era of the Washington Consensus. State terror was no longer necessary to apply it. The strategy of repression was replaced by the strategy of unemployment and social exclusion—the economic disappearance of people. In thirty years, industrial production declined by almost 50 percent, which represented, among other things, the loss of 600,000 jobs.[14]

By the end of 2000, according to a study conducted by the Economy Ministry, the country's ten biggest employers included four supermarkets, one fast-food chain, and one private security company. That is, low-quality jobs with little stability. The industrial sector, with the exception of the Ledesma sugar mill and the Arcor food corporation, did not appear among the top thirty employers. For example, McDonald's employed twice as many workers as the Repsol-YPF oil company.[15]

This is how the middle class began its massive fall to below the poverty line.

And the poor, below the starvation line.

Then came Fernando de la Rúa, a caricature of the worst of Alfonsín and the worst of Menem. He ended up declaring a state of siege and hearing the thunder of the *cacerolas*.[16]

To sum up: In 1974, Argentina had a distribution of wealth similar to many developed countries. The magnitude of the gap between the poorest sector and the richest was twelve times. The 2003 figures mark the gap between the poorest and the richest as fifty times greater. According to the explanation of specialist Artemio López, this indicates that "the bulk of the population transferred to the top the equivalent of 15 billion dollars annually."[17]

◆ ◆ ◆

With chants of "*que se vayan todos*" (they all must go) as the soundtrack, and a country reduced to institutional rubble as the backdrop, we can start to put names to this story.

The first: Juan Navarro.

In the 1990s he was held up as a paradigm of success. He was named businessman of the year in 1997. Three adjectives were used to describe him: successful, ambitious, and audacious. He was also called guru, talented financier, and brilliant executive. It was said that he was creating a new business culture. His empire: the Exxel Group, an investment fund that controlled the destinies of seventy-three companies and 40,000 employees.

"With no inherited fortune, it can be said that he built, at lightning speed, the third most powerful private economic group in Argentina, with 3.8 billion dollars in sales by the end of 1999," journalists Silvia Naishtat and Pablo Maas wrote in a biography of Navarro in *El Cazador*.

As the story goes, on March 17, 1992, Juan Navarro convinced the Oppenheimer & Company banks to help him build an investment fund. A few months later they sent him a check for $47 million dollars. He spent $22 million in the purchase of the Ciabasa and Poett companies (in the northern province of San Juan) and the aerosol division of the government-owned Repsol-YPF oil company. In less than sixty days he sold these companies to the multinational Clorox for $95 million.

For his second fund he collected $155 million. He purchased private health-care providers and provincial electric companies. For his subsequent funds he dispensed with Oppenheimer. It has since been unclear where his money comes from. "When the Anti-laundering Investigative Commission asked the North American funds that Navarro had listed as his investors if they were, in fact, Exxel associates, the majority denied it or remained silent," said Graciela Ocaña, House representative and member of the Commission.

One fact to keep in mind: One member of the Exxel Group's board of directors was the ex-ambassador of the United States to Argentina, Terence Todman.

Question: How did Exxel purchase so many companies?

Answer: Though leverage.

Explanation: "The companies would take out excessive loans, taking advantage of the U.S.'s low interest rates. They were bridge loans to pay off their own purchase. Once in charge of the business, the company would issue bonds guaranteed by the firm's assets. With the sale of the bonds he would cancel the loans."[18]

What did this mean?

That Navarro would obtain a multimillion dollar bank draft, or advance, to buy the companies. Once in his hands, that advance turned into a loan that the purchased company was forced to accept, offering its assets as a guarantee. This way, healthy companies would begin under new management with a huge and unpayable debt.

This is how the parliamentary report of the Anti-laundering Investigative Commission described how the Exxel Group operated: "When Exxel sets out to buy a company it secures two things: investors from abroad to contribute capital and a bank to advance it part of the purchase price as a short term credit. Once it has the company in its power, Exxel issues bonds under the company's name for a substantial amount (making it super-indebted) and mortgages all its assets as a guarantee of the bond's payment. In short, they buy a company—largely—with the company's own money."

◆ ◆ ◆

The Commission explains how Navarro hated the personal, family-owned business management style of the companies he bought.

That's why his first measure was to tear up the organizational chart. He would give the top positions to young, aggressive executives, who should, under no circumstance—he would say—keep their positions for more than three years. For this reason, he paid them extra.

"Many people wonder where Exxel's money comes from. A huge range of theories have been spun about the origin of those funds—from being part of Yabrán's[19] economic empire to being an investment of ex-president Carlos Menem. None of this was proven in this investigation. But one thing is for sure—at least part of the money comes out of the taxpayers' pocket.... The companies acquired by the funds, which then mortgage their assets, stop paying capital gains tax because their interest payments are deductible from that tax. The fiscal cost of these deductions therefore falls on the taxpayers, who don't enjoy a similar benefit. Interest on homeowners' mortgages, for example, is not deductible from the capital gains tax. But for funds like Exxel, the interest on the loans with which they buy companies is."[20]

In 2000 the Exxel Group accumulated 4.5 billion dollars in assets.

Two years later, its securities portfolio was worth a meager $300 million.

In late 2003 this was the status of its main companies:

Norte Supermarkets: In 1996 the Exxel Group bought Norte for 440 million dollars from its founder, Alberto Guil, paying mainly with bank debts and bonds sold in international markets. Two years later, the French chain Promodes bought 49 percent of Norte from Navarro's fund for 420 million dollars. Promodes had few executives in Argentina, and the ones it had were busy expanding their discount store, Día, in greater Buenos Aires. This meant that Norte was still managed by Exxel. One year later Norte bought the Tía chain from the De Narváez family and Deutsche Bank for 630 million dollars. Norte-Tía became an industry leader, with an average $2 billion in revenue per year. When the supermarket chain was

No Comment

In May 2003, federal human rights official Eduardo Mondino (Defensor del Pueblo) requested reports from several national government agencies on activities that were taking place surrounding recovered factories. The conclusions from the responses are as follows:

"The federal government had not addressed this issue and, in some cases, did not even know of its existence. The only government agency that seems to have taken note is the National Institute of Cooperatives and Social Economy (INAES), but it is also the one that has received the most criticism from the cooperatives regarding its functioning and its slowness in issuing licenses."

Mondino's report reproduces two responses to illustrate this. One, from the Ministry of Justice: "There is no program or proposal set up to organize the government's plans in conjunction with other agencies for the recovered factories, their workers, and their families." Another, from the office of the Cabinet: "There are no precedents for this issue." The Health Ministry, on the other hand, asked: "Is the National Movement of Recovered Companies (MNER) officially recognized? If so, how does it work?"

sold in April 2001 to the French firm Carrefour, it had accumulated 2 billion dollars in liabilities and a financial debt of $350 million.

Interbaires (operator of airport duty-free shops): Until December 1997 it was part of the empire of the late Alfredo Yabrán along with OCA, Ocasa, and Edcadassa. In a controversial move, the Exxel group paid $120 million for 80 percent of the company's duty-free stores operation. In November of 2002 it was taken over by its main creditor, the Deutsche Bank, because it could no longer pay its debt, estimated at $40 million. London Supply, a partnership formed by the Taratuty and Monteiro Branca families (the latter of Brazilian origin), bought it in March of 2003 for $20 million.

Fargo (food company): Founded by Carlos Preiti, controlled 60 percent of the market when it was sold for 140 million dollars. In February of 2003 Preiti himself returned to his old company, summoned by the trust formed by the firm's creditors, headed by the Deutsche Bank. The company had accumulated $150 million in debt.

Havanna (the makers of Argentina's best *alfajores*[21]): Acquired by the Exxel Group in March 1998. The founding families received 85 million dollars for a company that, at that time, had $15 million in revenue, an annual profit of $8 million, and no debt. Four years later, it held $32 million in liabilities. Its creditors: a group of banks headed by Deutsche Bank, Citibank, and Banco Rio. In October of 2003, executives of the Desarrollo y Gestión investment fund purchased Havanna from the Exxel Group for 5.5 million dollars cash and $12 million in refinanced bank credits. They included Guillermo Stanley and Carlos Giovanelli, former Citibank executives, and Chrystian Colombo, Rúa's former cabinet chief.

Musimundo (CD and video store chain): In May 1998, the Exxel Group offered Natalio Garber's family $230 million. When it called a creditors' meeting in late 2001, it owed $206 million. Its principal creditors: Citibank and Galicia (approximately $70 million between the two), the Brazilian Bozano and Supervielle. These banks kept Musimundo's stocks.

OCA (postal company): OCA, the private postal company that was the flagship of the Yabrán group, was acquired by the Exxel Group in December of 1997 for 450 million dollars. Drowning in debt, it was taken over by a bank syndicate headed by Deutsche Bank and Citibank. In February of 2004, OAC was sold for 32 million dollars in cash to the U.S. investment fund Advent, with the obligation to confront $280 million of debt.

MasterCard: Lost its Argentine operating license.

IBG (retail clothing chain, licensee for the brands Lacoste, Polo/Ralph Lauren, Paula Cahen d'Anvers, Coniglio, Kenzo): When a creditors' meeting was called, its debt was $90 million. At the end of 2003, Exxel reached an agreement with its creditors. It got a 50 percent write-down and a fifteen-year time limit with a three-year grace period. Its principal creditors were the banks. On that date, Coniglio, the only brand that did not participate in the meeting, was sold to a group of soy producers headed by the Hinz family and construction businessman Jorge Greco. When Exxel bought it, it had sixty locations. When Exxel sold it, it had three.

◆ ◆ ◆

However, out of all the companies that the Exxel Group bought, the one we are interested in for this story is the smallest— the Freddo ice cream parlor.

Founded by an Italian immigrant, Freddo had a fifty-year history of leading the industry, offering a high-quality product at six locations. Freddo's five associates received an offer they could not refuse from the Exxel Group: $82 million.

The first measure Navarro's management took was to remodel all the locations.

The second, to lower the quality of its ingredients.

The third, to raise prices.

There was no fourth—the company had already gone bankrupt.

This is how, in the spring of 2001, the ice cream store became part of Banco Galicia's assets, a consequence of the 30 million dollars it had accumulated in debts. The bank called on the old owner, Juan José Guarracino, to rescue the company, launching a formula that would later be applied to many bankrupt companies after the banks took them over. The financial vultures call it the "Freddo model."

◆ ◆ ◆

The domino effect of Navarro's raid on Freddo also pulled down one of the company's suppliers. Ghelco, located in the Barracas neighborhood of Buenos Aires, was suddenly without one of its main clients. Some time later, hit by the recession and financial speculation, it too ended up bankrupt.

For the forty Ghelco workers, that meant rationing their wages; then, months without a paycheck; and finally, the company's shutdown, leaving them on the street and without recourse. The Bankruptcy Law had been modified during Carlos Menem's term, and workers were no longer considered privileged creditors.

The banks came first.

Unemployment at that time was at 22 percent.

Everyone at Ghelco knew what was in store for them—their average age was forty, they were highly specialized workers with families, debts, and bills that could not wait. They had nowhere to go and, with that conviction, they stayed.

◆ ◆ ◆

A green tent housed them for months outside the locked doors of the factory. Two police cars and a dozen officers guarded them.

In fact, it was a police officer who told them that a few months earlier, police had thrown workers out of a nearby factory, using clubs. "But they came back," he told them. "They formed a cooperative and walked back in."

The Ghelco workers went that very day to meet those other workers—at the Lavalán wool processing plant—who, in turn, took them to meet lawyer Luis Caro, who, on the spot, photocopied the eighty-four articles of a worker cooperative statute. They called it Vieytes.

This is how the story ends.

The factory was expropriated.

The workers, organized as the Vieytes Worker Cooperative, took charge and reopened it.

No one talks about Navarro anymore.

◆ ◆ ◆

Today the workers at what used to be Ghelco earn double their old wage. "The day we walked in, we didn't even have money to buy a bag of sugar. The guys from another cooperative—Unión y Fuerza—gave us a loan for some ingredients and for the electricity bill, and that's how we started. With our first sale, the first thing we did was pay them back. We didn't even have money to eat, but the debts came first, and we were proud of being able to pay them."

This is where another story begins.

If you walk into the Ghelco cooperative now, you see the following scene in the machine room:

Along the wall are the mixers and grinders, working full blast.

In the middle of the room, in three lines, are forty school desks. "They're for the assemblies. They said we couldn't make all our decisions by assembly because we would have to stop working. So someone got the idea that it would be best to meet in the machine room, so those who were on the clock could work, discuss, and vote."

The workers display their work proudly—machines and direct democracy. They smile, they look relaxed, confident, content, complete.

That's change.

◆ ◆ ◆

The Ghelco story serves to illustrate one of the most interesting movements that has emerged from the heat of the Argentine crisis. It establishes the connection that is essential to understanding this process—that without Navarro, there is no Vieytes Cooperative.

Without dirty money, impunity, and capital flight, there are no recovered factories.

Navarro is the front for the anonymous capital that can, with a keystroke, move investments from one place to another without ever having to explain itself, much less suffer the consequences of its actions. Its power in its current form—no longer in any one place, but with a capacity for "flight, escape, the complete rejection of any territorial restraint and its bothersome corollaries of construction and maintenance of order, responsibility for its consequences, and the need to assume its costs."[22]

◆ ◆ ◆

In May 2002, during a session of the Chamber of Deputies in the National Congress [the Argentine parliament], one representative summed up the state of things:

"We've seen how a vulture capital fund that fabricates debt, takes over companies with short-term loans and takes down firms like Pan Fargo, Alfajores Havanna, Supermercados Norte or Heladerias Freddo. What law provides for all this? With all due respect, we need to study modern economics a little more. Because economic crimes are no longer about a bounced check or a faked balance sheet, but about electronic crimes, complicated crimes of billion-dollar currency transfers, in which untold masses of money strip countries bare or make certain people rich.... What is the role of Congress? What we saw in the U.S. Senate, when they sat the country's main bankers down to warn them about money laundering from the drug trade, arms trafficking, terrorism and gambling, and the fact that the legislation had to be changed. This is what this Congress should do after hearing the report from the

Anti-laundering Investigative Commission. That is, change legislation to avoid these conflicts."[23]

This quotation is printed here for one purpose—to illustrate the Argentine Parliament's awareness of these maneuvers and the practical consequences of that knowledge.

The House did not pass any new reform that day.

It did, however, repeal the Law of Economic Subversion (the law under which more than fifty CEOs of local and multinational banks had been charged with illegal capital flight), at the explicit request of the IMF.

It is this power, backed by a criminal conspiracy of global speculative capitalism (managed by the international credit organizations), an accomplice state, and a corrupt national bourgeoisie—this ferocious and decadent cocktail—that produces the huge vacuum, the space where those who know that no one will rescue them invent the only way to fight back.

◆ ◆ ◆

We repeat: power is no longer a place, but a capacity.

Bauman defined it like this:

"It's the pencil that draws the line between what is legitimate and illegitimate. The right to establish the limit between legitimate (admissible) and illegitimate (inadmissible) coercion is the first objective of any power struggle."[24]

The protagonists of this story have learned how to snatch the pencil and literally write their own conditions of legitimacy.

This tension doesn't disappear, in most cases, it's still present.

To start, it is expressed in the legal situation of each reclaimed factory. Very few have taken ownership of the company's property through some kind of compensation to the previous owner, normalizing the ownership of the title to the business. The vast majority remain in a true legal limbo, as is the case with Zanón, whose workers have been able to stop repeated eviction attempts thanks to massive community support. In other cases, such as that of Brukman (see chapter 2), after three forcible evictions and a tenacious resistance, the bankruptcy judge finally indicted the previous owners, and the Buenos Aires legislature granted the expropriation of the factory after reviewing the workers' plan to reactivate it. In a few cases, the combined pressure of the movement and certain legislators has achieved temporary solutions, such as the expropriation of a company's land and machinery for two-year periods.

The legal processes are dynamic and changing. Generally, the workers begin the legal proceedings by offering to rent the factory. A detailed reading of the Bankruptcy Law gave rise to this strategy, since it states that all efforts to guarantee payment to the creditors must be exhausted. Then they request the expropriation of the machines and finally, the expropriation of the property. This last stage can only be accomplished by the passage of a specific law, so it no longer depends on the presiding judge, but on the local legislature. Here the workers apply direct pressure, going so far as to camp out in front the legislators' offices in their overalls, surrounded by their families.

So far, most factories have been handed over only provisionally. And absent the political will to reform the Bankruptcy Law into an efficient, universal, and permanent tool, the battle will be waged round by round, factory by factory, case by case.

Power is not about to let go of the pencil.

◆ ◆ ◆

For the weak institutions of Argentina's capricious democracy, these factories pose a political and social dilemma for which they don't have an answer. The answers they've given so far have been provisional and pried from them by the tenacity of the struggle, the validity of the demands, the flagrant illegality of the situations that gave rise to those demands, and the absence of policies that create decent jobs. It was not government officials, judges, or experts who showed these workers how to make their claims clearly, nor how to find the solutions that address them. It was their own hard-won experience that showed them the way out of each jam.

Perhaps the origin can be found in the first factory to be expropriated. The Yaguané meatpacking plant's former owner was Alberto Samid, a man close to Menem, indicted for multimillion dollar fraud of the federal treasury. Under worker control, the plant came to lead the beef industry in export revenues, but the workers barely earned enough to eat. Their mistake: by legally taking ownership of the company, they also inherited its millions in debt, which had to be paid punctually. To avoid this kind of inherited burden, the workers came up with a new structure—they organized themselves into a worker cooperative.

◆ ◆ ◆

Why a worker cooperative? For several important reasons.

In the first place, because it allows workers to legally clarify that any of the old owner's debts, crimes, or penalties do not belong to the group that will now take charge of production.

In addition, worker cooperatives recognize the workforce itself as sufficient capital to start a business.

Nonetheless, the true original motive was practical—registering a corporation in Argentina costs a minimum of 300 dollars. A worker cooperative, on the other hand, costs only $45. All it takes is for six members to provide the equivalent of 10 percent of the minimum wage as set by the government.

The licensing for cooperatives is also different. Cooperatives are accredited by the National Institute of Associations and Social Economy (INAES), a national body that was practically lifeless until these cooperatives came along and found in it a way to avoid a much more bureaucratic (and expensive) institution. INAES, whose president, José Martinez de Hoz, economy minister under the dictatorship, had crippled it with restrictions and turned it into a museum.

Over time, in the course of their battles for recognition, workers also managed to transform their cooperatives into tax shelters, since they are exempt from capital gains taxes and, in many districts, municipal taxes as well.

◆ ◆ ◆

The line drawn by that pencil snatched from the hand of power can also be found in the cooperatives' statutes—especially in two of them. The first one has to do with earnings. It no longer speaks in terms of salaries, but about profit distribution. In general, the worker cooperatives tend to share income equally, though in some cases there is a wage scale according to responsibility. Nonetheless, in practice, and especially during the first months—when earnings are scarce—they take the needs of the members into account and distribute the money according to their own order of priorities: number of children, ability to survive on other sources of income, age, and seniority, among other factors.

The second statute has to do with the dissolution of a cooperative. Members that retire do not have compensation rights. Since the co-op's value is based on work, once you stop working, you stop earning. And if the entire cooperative dissolves, its statutes must state the destination of its remaining funds, which must be donated.

INAES requires that every worker cooperative appoint a management committee consisting of a president, vice president, and treasurer. Nevertheless, in most cases the statutes are written so that these posts have no set term lengths and also so that they are subject to recall by an assembly of the workers. The assembly is thereby established as the highest decision-making body, and can be convened at any time. In many assemblies, there is not even a set agenda— anyone can propose a topic and the others must hear him or her out. This is how the workers debate strategy and business deals, account balances, and legal tactics. If necessary, they bring in advisors (lawyers, engineers, accountants) to explain technical issues, but afterwards, decisions are made by consensus or by a show of hands.

While it is true that most of these companies have been structured as worker cooperatives, during the movement's climax, some demanded nationalization under workers' control, a model that attracted much more support from outside the movement than from the movement itself. In fact, nationalization has shown itself to be a utopian goal under a state that, at best, shows contempt toward the movement. To date, there have been two examples of nationalization under workers' control. One is the Medrano Health Clinic, taken over by the government of the city of Buenos Aires in December 2003, after two years of worker occupation and excellent management. Months of inaction followed the city government's decision to take over, and then it decided to reassign the workers to various other government agencies. The clinic remains closed, despite the government's commitment to open a senior citizens' center there.

The other is the case of the Nogaró Hotel, in the province of San Juan. For almost two years it was run by a worker cooperative, until the provincial government decided to step in. It kept the co-op workers on contract for six months and then put the hotel up for sale.

◆ ◆ ◆

The economic viability of the worker cooperatives has to be considered case by case. First of all, much depends on the situation the workers start with. Many can only function *"à façon"*—a system in which the client advances part of the payment so that the cooperative has capital to buy the raw materials needed for the order. This is the system they invented to overcome the limitations imposed by their lack of credit and financing.

And this is how they have been able to get their companies back into production—through their own efforts, in spite of the challenges caused by their lack of training in administration and commercial matters, the distrust of the old clients, and police and legal harassment. In time, some companies have gone on to export or even lead their markets, while others still find themselves right where they started.

In any case, through the experience of worker management, the workers have discovered the real reasons behind their companies' bankruptcies. And they have reached a conclusion: what bankrupts them are employer costs.

Employer costs do not just refer to the huge slice that the owners take, but also to a whole series of costs that have to be covered by production: bloated managerial wages and bonuses, commissions, trips, chauffeurs, and travel expenses, consultant fees for restructurings that inevitably point to labor costs as the reason for the profit deficit.

This new understanding adopted by the workers—arising from a reality of which little news has reached economic academia—places responsibility on the other end. This concept of employer costs reveals that all those expenses are unnecessary under worker control, placing the responsibility for bankruptcy squarely on the old management. Interestingly, many of these factories are

Bankruptcy Law

Article 191 of the bankruptcy law stipulates, "authorization for keeping the company open will be given by a judge only in cases in which closure could result in a serious decline in value or if it would interrupt ongoing production." Judges have interpreted this provision with greater or lesser flexibility, but even in those cases resolved in favor of workers, rulings have been forced by dramatic circumstances—unemployment, fraud, millions in back pay owed to workers. A new demand is to change the law to preserve the continuity of employment. The Federal Ombudsman has said, "How is it possible that everyone involved—workers, judges, and legislators—move back and forth between legality and illegality without doing anything to fix the situation?" That question still hasn't been answered.

now being studied by management experts who are reevaluating business practices that were considered gospel in the 1990s.

◆ ◆ ◆

Every recovered company knows that its survival depends on whatever legitimacy and community ties it can manage to build. Its defense lies in the conviction of its workers, but also in the support it garners from neighbors, neighborhood assemblies, human rights organizations, and political parties—in that order. Once under worker control, recognizing their precarious legal standing, some factories imitated IMPA, the pioneering aluminum products cooperative, and opened community cultural centers on their premises. IMPA did it as an act of self-defense. Faced with the threat of a violent eviction at the hands of the police, it opened its doors for activities such as theater, movies, classes, tutoring, and lectures. Most activities were free and organized by university students or members of neighborhood assemblies. In this way, they guaranteed that the factory would be occupied during the nights and weekends, considered the factory's most vulnerable times. Today, thanks to pressure on the government from the IMPA workers and their supporters, they have been able to establish accredited schools to teach metalworking trades.

In this way, the pencil has crossed out principles that Power holds as unassailable truths:

Supremacy of private property at any cost.

The government as the only possible arena for resolving social conflict.

The necessity of relying on a managerial class to organize production.

The proof that none of these statements is inevitable is evident each time workers tell their stories. At the Grissinopoli factory, for example, one worker remembers the hardest thing he had to face. It wasn't taking to the streets, enduring hunger, confronting the police, arguing with the judge, or lobbying the legislators. What challenged him most was convincing his co-workers that they were perfectly capable of running the factory themselves, "They thought I was crazy." When the day finally came that the machines started again, they cried. And they hugged him.

Being their own bosses gave the workers a new image of themselves.

They knew then that they would never be the same again.

That it was not their lives that had changed, but their destinies.

◆ ◆ ◆

In an old book on labor law, French specialist Alain Supiot notes that the first use of the word "labor" refers to a woman's burden during childbirth. He alludes, fundamentally, to that act that intertwines pain and creation and contains nothing less than the very mystery of human destiny.[25]

It can be said that the destiny of the workers of the nearly 170 recovered factories in Argentina has already been written:

"The splitting up of society into a small class, immoderately rich, and a large class of wage-laborers devoid of all property, brings it about that this society smothers in its own superfluidity, while the great majority of its members are scarcely, or not at all, protected from extreme want.

This condition becomes every day more absurd and more unnecessary. It must be gotten rid of; it can be gotten rid of."[26]

This is what Frederich Engels said on April 30, 1891. Some

113 years later, the workers of Zanón, in southern Argentina, eliminated something.

They baptized their creation with a name straight out of a dream: *Fabrica Sin Patrón*, "factory without a boss."

This story and this change belong to them, and others like them.

◆ ◆ ◆

The following pages are the product of two long years of venturing into that other reality that is flourishing outside the media spotlight—and sometimes, even in spite of it. We try to testify to the richness of this movement, its diversity and contradictions, and to give back some of all that we learned along the way. We are indebted to this story and to these workers for the formation of our own legal entity as a cooperative,[27] among other things. But, above all, for the questioning, and even the doubts about how to survive and grow, and even whether it is necessary to do so.

Finally, we owe it to them to read the following sentence:

"Beyond our diverse beliefs, often so different, and sometimes fiercely confronted, we all desire to live with dignity and without fear, without humiliation, so we may find happiness. This constitutes a common ground firm and broad enough on which to commence building solidarity in action and conception."[28]

And to mean it.

With energy, patience, and trust.

Chapter One

Zanón

A Deal to Live By

Zanón is the largest reclaimed factory, with a model worker-run management. It has created jobs, conquered its market, and won the support of its entire community to defend it against constant threats of eviction. Amen.

Zanón is one of the strangest factories around. Going inside is to immerse yourself in the thunder of incomprehensible machines, meticulous robots, and smiling people that do something that some courts have declared a crime: work.

When the thunder subsides, background music can be heard. One of the favorites is still a song by the Argentine group Bersuit Vergarabat: "Un pacto para vivir" ("A Deal to Live By").

Strange factory. Zanón was consistently profitable, but its owners provoked one conflict after another in order to lay off workers, restructure the plant, and further increase its profitability. (Recall the tale of Aesop in 600 BC, about the owner of a hen that laid golden eggs. This fable has not made the rounds in Argentine business circles.)

The union supported the owners. This backroom deal clashed with the almost innocent obstinance of the workers, who could not believe that the company they had worked a lifetime for would do them such injustice. Luis Zanón, a smiling man of false intentions and friends (the most notorious, perhaps, being Carlos Menem), ended up abandoning the plant. Later, Judge Norma Rivero declared this an offensive lockout.

That was when the judicial tango began.

(An explanation for the uninitiated: the Argentine judicial system has more faces than a die. Sometimes everything depends on chance, although it is also known that those who run this system use loaded dice).

Zanón's main business became taking back the plant from the workers, who fought back—successfully—on five occasions. Meanwhile, two other things made Zanón one of the strangest factories around.

First, the workers fought back while simultaneously increasing production. They increased the workforce by 80 percent. Second, they created a cooperative so that the courts would recognize them as a separate entity from the old Zanón. The plant is now called FaSinPat (from Fábrica Sin Patrón, "Factory Without a boss").

They are systematically harassed on all sides: by the courts, the police, the politicians and the mafia. Again, it is the same die— everything depends on if you get lucky. Or unlucky.

Veteran Criminals

In what ways has the new Zanón been criminalized?

"In every way, and from day one," says Raúl Godoy, well

known for wearing his trademark cap. He has become a symbol of the workers' demands. "From the start they accused us of being trespassers. We took the factory in October 2001. In November, we blocked the road. So [the authorities] pressed charges against me. They used photos as evidence—drawing little circles around the people they were looking for. It's funny—they used a TV clip that shows a huge assembly on the road, voting to block it. There are people from the University of Comahue, teachers, the MTD (Movement of Unemployed Workers) of Neuquén, the people of Zanón, people from the community ... but they only prosecuted me as the supposed instigator. A highly selective persecution began."

Godoy is a member of the Socialist Workers Party (PTS), a party that came in last in the 2003 Neuquén state elections. Having been unable to capitalize on the prestige of the Zanón struggle, or on that of its most prominent public figure, Godoy, its showing was below all the other left-leaning parties. Godoy has earned the respect of nonpartisan and apolitical citizens, but Zanón's assembly voted against any of its workers running in elections.

Pressure and Persecution

Godoy faced threats from a police official named Herrera, but the courts didn't pay attention. Police also flashed weapons threateningly at Godoy's young daughters and trashed their house in a robbery described by neighbors as a "commando operation."

Another key event was a robbery and kidnapping by two criminals who escaped from the Unit 11 prison. The *Río Negro* newspaper described them as "two veteran criminals." The leader was "the *Gordo Valor* of Neuquén,"[1] said Godoy, referring to the type of criminals whose distinction from the police is infinitely small. His name: Nelson Gómez Tejada. His sidekick was Juan Antonio Gómez. Veterans of crime, not because of their age (37 and 25 years old, respectively), but because of their records.

Both escapees arrived at the house of Zanón worker Miguel Vázquez. Neighbors reported suspicious movements because they saw Gómez on the roof cutting the electric and telephone wires. The police arrived, chatted amiably with Gómez Tejada, and left. Both Gómez and Gómez Tejada were fugitives from Unit 11, with warrants out for their arrest, but the police, perhaps in a humanitarian gesture, did not apprehend them.

Armed, Gómez Tejada entered the house, held the family hostage, and stole the money that was to pay the Zanón workers the following day—more than 20,000 pesos. Another worker, Miguel Papatryphonos, came to pick up Vázquez in his Fiat Uno. Gómez Tejada kidnapped both men and stole the Fiat Uno. The accumulation of criminal complaints pressured the police into apprehending Gómez Tejada. But a few weeks later, he escaped from Unit 11 again. He was like a kid playing hooky from school.

Godoy says, "They were later tried, but their case was dismissed due to lack of evidence. And they were fugitives from prison when they committed the robbery!" The money never turned up. *Río Negro* wrote, in its coverage of the trial, how the prosecution "questioned the victims as if they were the perpetrators." The workers ended up throwing eggs, tomatoes and rotten cabbages at the courthouse, symbolizing their opinion of the judicial system.

Tapped Cell Phones

There's more. Including a failed attempt at kidnapping Carlos Acuña, Zanón's press spokesman (he saved himself by screaming as they tried to push him into a car), telephone threats, mysterious cars—nothing new in Argentina.[2] None of the workers' criminal complaints to authorities went anywhere. The judicial system makes protesting a crime, but it doesn't always make crime a crime.

Another commando operation was carried out in December 2003, when gunmen armed with shotguns showed up at Zanón, walked into the sales area, tied up the workers there, distributed a generous round of blows with the butts of their shotguns, stole the day's earnings, and fled comfortably and fearlessly in the direction of the police station.

The persecution also exhibited technological innovations, such as cell phone tapping. Godoy says, "It's become routine for us. We're talking in a meeting, they call a coworker who is outside and play him our conversation, everything we're talking about. They use your own cell phone as a radio. I receive a message, according to the caller ID it's from a co-worker, but instead they play me the recording of a meeting. At this point, it makes us laugh. The other day I told someone, 'Get your phone out of here, you idiot, you're transmitting the whole meeting.' This is completely normal here."

The workers have cases pending in the provincial court, local tribunals, reviewing magistrates, labor courts, and legislatures. "We never know where the shot will come from," Godoy points out.

The next surprise came in 2004 at the Buenos Aires Bankruptcy Court, when the worker delegation ran into Luis Zanón himself, who, besides his smile, had other hangers-on—representatives from the World Bank and another international bank, as well as former bureaucrats displaced from the ceramics union. The banks are Zanón's creditors and the unionists belong to the breed that has gotten fat thanks to good relationships with the owners.

Godoy reflects, "This shows the magnitude of what we're up against. The stakes are high because many planets are aligning against us, and in general, [aligning] against the reclaimed factories. They want to see you on your knees, to show that workers are good for nothing, least of all for running a business."

Where's the Money?

Maybe it is true. Maybe workers are no good at running companies in the style that the international banks and the owner corps advocate. Examples: the Zanón workers gave the uion bureaucracy the boot (instead of fattening it), got a factory that the bosses had abandoned up and running, and rather than laying people off, they actually created jobs.

The plant covers 80,000 square meters in area and occupies nine hectares in all. A tour through those buildings, extending as far as the eye can see, shows machine display screens speckled with matrix-style green dots, men and women focused on their work (but also allowing themselves the time to chat) huge metal claws, mechanical caterpillars with tongs that grab and pile ceramic pieces. Glue guns for cardboard boxes, metal plates that move like iron hands and package it all. Farther down, also inside the plant, there are huge funnels, four or five stories high, mixing a muddy substance. An internal transport vehicle passes by, sliding down

Making Resistance a Crime

In Argentina, as of late 2004, more than 4,000 men and women, including many workers who fought to reclaim their factories or companies, were tied up in the criminal justice system. These are the legal consequences of participating in roadblocks and other activities to save jobs, social benefits, education, and health-care, among other rights. In spite of the Kirchner administration's pledges to put an end to these criminal prosecutions through amnesty, the government "forgot" about their original promise and continued prosecuting activists—"with the penal code in hand," according to Interior Minister Aníbal Fernández. As a result, the trend of criminalizing social protest got a major legal boost—arbitrarily arresting demonstrators, and incarcerating them while they await trial on charges for crimes that result in no convictions.

the tracks like a train, setting off an alarm. Nobody is driving it. The smooth sounds of "Un pacto para vivir" drift through the air.

The cardboard boxes say "FaSinPat," the name brand on the ceramics.

The Web page www.fasinpat.com.ar displays the models and designs produced at the plant, such as the once-fired ceramics (there are thirteen lines, among them, the "Mapuche"—a local indigenous tribe—and the "Worker" lines), the porcelain, and polished porcelains (another twelve lines). These latter products place FaSinPat, potentially, at a level where it can compete on the international market, since, in fact, Zanón, before beheading the golden goose, exported to Australia and ten European countries. One of its projects, according to worker Christian Moya, was to focus the plant exclusively on porcelain production. "It's the top of the line in floors on an international level, a polished, glossy floor. We're the only Latin American plant with three polishers, and the only one that fabricates everything, from the primary materials to the finished product. It's inexplicable and absurd how, with that potential, they took things to the extreme of ruining it," he says.

Some hypotheses include that Mr. Zanón was transferring his profits abroad. Others suspected that he threw them into the speculative gambles of the 1990s financial markets. But all agree that both these possibilities were common practices during the reigns of Menem and de la Rúa.

The tour continues. In the managers' room there is an assembly area (the cell phones stay outside) and posters stating: "We demand genuine work, they give us lead bullets and repression" and "*Clarín:* infantry journalism."[3] There are elementary schoolchildren's drawings—images of workers working, something that has turned into magical realism in broad swatches of Argentina.

The Soccer Ruse

Miguel Ramírez and Reinaldo Giménez are two of the factory's young veterans. They drink *mate*[4] and replay the story. Until 1998 everything seemed to be going relatively well. Giménez says, "Zanón was making 44 million dollars in profits annually. In '94 it reached $67 million. But they started cutting back on materials and supplies. They even took away our working material, all with the union's complicity."

The Neuquén Ceramics Workers' and Employees' Union (SOECN) and the Zanón internal commission were controlled by the Montes brothers, who were in bed with the bosses.

Ramírez says, "Zanón was a phony. He would come a couple times a year, tour the factory, and pat someone on the back. That person was then fired. We figured out that was his way of pointing out the ones he didn't like." Another typical strategy, he relates, "If they wanted to lay off five workers, they would announce twenty layoffs. The union would pretend to intervene, fight and negotiate, and would end up saying, '*Well, we got them to reinstate fifteen.*' And that's how they would get rid of the five the boss wanted to can."

In 1998, the Brown List (la Lista Marrón), a slate of liberal union militants, managed to defeat the old union bureaucracy in internal commission elections.

Conditions at the factory continued to deteriorate and displaced workers took on a policing role with respect to their coworkers.

How do you organize in that environment? Carlos Acuña says, "It occurred to us to organize a soccer tournament outside the factory. There are fourteen sectors, each with their own team, who elect a delegate to go to the tournament-organizing meetings. That's where we took the opportunity to discuss things." This clandestine mechanism worked as a mode of internal organization and communication (and the tournament was good, too).

For example, in the company there was talk of a crisis, but at the tournament meetings the workers pooled data and made calculations. "What crisis, if twenty trucks go out per day, they have 25 percent of the internal [i.e., Argentine] market and export to who knows how

Academic Networking

The Interdisciplinary University Support Group (GUIA) is a network of universities that have signed agreements to provide technical assistance and training to FaSinPat, the Zanón ceramics cooperative. In the case of the University of Buenos Aires (UBA) School of Economic Sciences, the agreement establishes a coordination unit formed by Felisa Miceli (president of Banco Nacional) and professor Abraham Gak, founder of the group of economists that produced the Phoenix Plan.* Professor Pablo Levin, director of the Center for the Study of Planning and Economic Development (CEPLAD) at UBA, completes the group. There are also agreements with the UBA School of Natural Sciences and the University of Comahue that have supported worker management since the beginning.

* The Phoenix Plan (el Plan Fénix) was an economic blueprint, produced in September 2001 by leading economists at the University of Buenos Aires, for reviving the Argentinian economy through Keynesian measures, focusing on policies for social welfare and national development.

many countries? What crisis, if they have state tax breaks, loans, and every imaginable benefit because Zanón lives in Sobisch's shadow?" Acuña asked himself. Sobisch is the Governor of Neuquén who says openly that he considers himself a corporate lobbyist.

Giving Your Life for the Boss

In 2000, the internal situation took a turn for the worse. Paychecks were late, and in June, twenty-year-old Daniel Ferrás died of a respiratory-related heart attack inside the factory. Moya says,

"That's when we saw that the first aid room was just a façade—even the oxygen tube was empty."

Ramírez states, "They didn't even give us uniforms. They didn't pay us. Folks started to see that everything was rotten, and on top of it came Daniel's death." This unleashed a nine-day battle that calmed only when Zanón began issuing paychecks on time. In December 2000 the factory's workers dealt the bosses a new blow. Accomplishing something that hardly ever happens in Argentine trade unions, union militants defeated the old bureaucracy to take control of the union, with Raúl Godoy becoming the general secretary. In 2001 the conflict worsened. Ramírez recounts the sequence of events, "They suspended people, the strikes began, and everything went to hell."

Giménez recounts what he thinks was Zanón's big mistake, summing up his theory on worker-owner psychology: "There are people who have been working here for twenty or twenty-five years, people who didn't miss a day, who lived for Zanón. He [Zanón] would have caused a great division [among the workers] if he had said, 'I won't pay the union activists because they're lazy,' or for whatever reason. But he put everyone in the same boat, and the workers with the longest tenures said, 'This scumbag should have paid me. I gave him my life, but he has no feelings, no compassion, and he makes no distinctions.'"

The conflict turned into a strike. Workers set up tents outside Zanón. They began organizing pickets, marches, and demonstrations. On his end, Zanón received loans from the provincial government to pay the workers' wages, but he kept the loans and didn't pay the workers. Meanwhile, the local media ran a story about Zanón's participation in charity dinners in Buenos Aires, along with Domingo Cavallo, Amalita Fortabat, Franco Macri[5] and owners of some privatized companies, where they paid 10,000 dollars a plate to [presumably] fight poverty.

On October 10, 2001, facing what already constituted abandonment of the factory on the owner's part, the workers occupied the plant. Giménez says, "That's when the situation broke loose, and the managerial hierarchy had to go. We made them leave. We told the managers that we couldn't allow things to continue this way. We didn't pressure anyone, and many of us decided to stay. A member of the company's security team stayed as well, but never got paid either and ended up leaving."

Says Moya, "We organized communal kitchens, held events, anything to survive. But the factory was a cemetery. Absolutely dead."

The workers received support from the community, schools, local clubs, their own neighbors. Even inmates at the local jail sent them their food rations.

They picketed awhile, but then regretted it when they discovered that their idea of protesting ended up isolating them. "The people on the other side were workers too, just like us," they remember. This is typical of many discussions at Zanón—they pledge formal solidarity to the *piqueteros*,[6] but they insist on differentiating themselves from them. Carlos Quiñimir states, "The people notice that we're not piqueteros, but heads of households." The prejudice against the piqueteros, perhaps unconscious, is not exclusive to the middle class.

Whose Factory Is It?

The workers' tools changed—they *became* the megaphone, the flier, using their own words.

They explained their situation to anyone who would listen. They would board buses and tell passengers their story during the ride. They used megaphones in different neighborhoods to introduce themselves to community members and spread the word about their situation and their actions. On the roads, instead of blocking traffic, they would pass out fliers to the drivers. "Many cars would stop and unload food that they had brought for us," said Giménez.

"The solidarity was tremendous," remembers Ramírez. "They sent us so much food we didn't know where to store it. We put packages of it together and sold them to raise money for the strike fund. There was a lot of support from the community and small businesses." Why so much support? Gímenez says, "We always said the factory isn't ours. We are using it, but it belongs to the community. They asked what we were doing and we explained that we aren't intolerant piqueteros, the kind armed with clubs. At most we used tires to block the road, and if someone had an accident we would help them. At an assembly, we made another decision. The workers said: we don't want to block traffic anymore. We decided to go out into the streets, but to explain, and explain more, because otherwise no one would understand what we were doing. They would think we were slackers."

In December 2001, a Zanón march in front of a government building was attacked by police whose commanders yelled, "Get the brown shirts!" There was no mistaking who to go after. At that event the workers protested by burning their pink slips.

In March 2002 the workers started the plant's operations again, as well as announcing a plan to nationalize the plant under worker control. Press spokesman Carlos Acuña says, "We know the factory is absolutely profitable, we continue to hire people, we pay all the bills, and the profits shouldn't go to us, or to the politicians and bosses, but to the community."

Media Provocateur

In his book *La política mirada desde arriba* (*Politics Seen from Above*), the sociologist Ricardo Sidicaro reviewed a large number of editorials published in the daily Argentine newspaper *La Nación* between 1909 and 1989. The newspaper was the voice of a group of conservatives that for decades used their role to lecture the Argentine ruling class. From the 1970s on, Sidicaro argues, in reality, there is no consistency in the media, nor are there political forces to whom they can continue giving their lectures. He wrote, "In a certain sense, *La Nación* editorials found no representatives, but, at the same time, the paper itself did not know where to go—to speak on behalf of a social tradition or on behalf of a corporation." Perhaps to overcome this disconnect, on the topic of the reclaimed enterprises, it speaks from both sides of its mouth. An example:

On March 4, 2004, an editorial directly attacked the reclaimed factories, calling for their liquidation and the expulsion of their workers. Attempting to respond to this attack, lavaca.org sent the following open letter to the paper's editors:

"*La Nación*, in its March 4th editorial, called for the destruction of the factories reclaimed by Argentine workers. In

Because they called for nationalization, the idea of a cooperative didn't interest them initially. Nevertheless, they formed FaSin-Pat as a transitory solution to take charge of Zanón.

They became a case study. Ramírez continues, "Cáritas[7] and

making its case, a series of falsehoods and ideological arguments were used.

The editorial recognizes that global financial institutions prefer that the joblessness problem be addressed with unemployment benefits and not with the creation of decent jobs. This argument reveals who *really* promotes, finances and supports dependency and social exclusion in Argentina. It concluded by publicly pressuring judges, demanding, "The Courts must urgently review their attitude to the occupation of businesses."

Taking into account the perilous financial situation of *La Nación*, and its drop in sales—both in newspapers sold and in advertising—and the even lower quality of its product, it stands to reason that it sympathizes with the fraudulent corporate officials—convicted in courts—who provoked this movement created by hardworking people who try to earn an honest living.

This defense of the indefensible is morally nauseating. Nevertheless, the nearly 10,000 jobs created by these factories run with the sweat and efficiency of their workers lead us to suggest something else: that *La Nación* is the intellectual author of whatever attack these workers suffer.

Buenos Aires, March 17, 2004.

Naomi Klein made movies about us. Delegations of people came from Italy, France, Bulgaria, Germany, the United States, Spain—from all over the place."

Living and Working Together

The assembly established some rules for the cooperative. Showing up fifteen minutes early and leaving work fifteen minutes after officially getting off, for example, so the workers can get updated on the latest news. Moya tells about when "a co-worker who was stealing" had to be fired. On the other hand, "one *compañero* had a drug addiction—we paid for his treatment and kept his job on hold for him."

Each worker decides his or her own lunch hour. Moya says, "Everyone knows their responsibilities. Some rules may even be similar to the old company's, but this is no boot camp." During lunch, one can see Godoy himself serving *milanesas*[8] to other workers or to astonished journalists.

What about the pace of production? Quiñimir, sipping on *mate* without stopping his department's machines (moving ceramic pieces to the ovens), describes, "When we had an owner, I couldn't talk the way we are right now. I couldn't even stop for a couple of minutes. Now I work calmly, with my conscience as my guide, and without a boss yelling that we have to reach the oh-so-important objective. Back then we ran very short oven cycles. It got down to twenty-eight minutes, when the recommended time is thirty-five or more, as we do it today."

What's the difference? "It was really easy to burn your hands and because of the speed of the machines, you couldn't stop them to make adjustments. You had to fix them while they were running, which led to many accidents. You could easily lose two or three fingers."

This could be taken to imply that things don't move at the speed of the hyperactive capitalism of recent history. Nonetheless, the workers have increased production, profits and the workforce—from 240 when they took over the factory to 400 in 2004.

The Left, the Assembly, and the Alternative

How far does the influence of political parties go in the assemblies? Quiñimir says, "The assembly is paramount. The parties play an important role, but they are subordinate to the overall assembly. There's no party that says 'this we do and this we don't.' There were some confrontations because we resisted anyone trying to negotiate the conflict, but in the process those roles were worked out. Leftist parties supported us during difficult times, but we didn't let that confuse us, nor did we let ourselves become directly influenced." What about Godoy? "Raúl is one of our co-workers, and the fact that he's a member of a party is another matter. The conflict forced us all to learn. You have to respect the worker and the party activist. They need each other. When something reaches an impasse, the assembly, which is the maximum authority, decides."

Alberto Esparza—his previous party affiliation a distant memory—adds, "The compañeros who deal with political issues also have to work the machines, and those in production have to be ready to take their places. If not, we make the mistake, no offense intended, of always looking to Raúl Godoy. It's an instinct of the Right to always look for a single leader. There are at least a hundred workers here capable of being delegates in any factory."

Alberto summarizes, "You could say there's a leftist leadership

here, that there's opposition to the capitalist system. But I think
the worst thing that could happen would be for this to turn into
something sectarian or partisan."

Carlos Acuña adds, "Raúl is in a party; he can bring his proposals. And, I—not belonging to any party—bring mine that I
have discussed with my family at home. We vote and decide. That
simplifies things for us, and makes it so we don't always have a political party's hat on." Carlos recognizes, "We've learned a lot from
the Left and the PTS, like they have learned a lot from us." For example? "That you can't come here with strange ideas, because they
just won't fly." What strange ideas? "Wanting to impose an
agenda, wanting to run the show. Here the group runs the show."

Alberto Esparza adds another political angle, "One can't detach
oneself from society and have a message demanding social justice that
reaches no one." Those sound like the words of a party activist. "I'm
not in any party, but I want to plant a seed here. You know, children,
students come here and ask how we did this. The first thing we did
was break the law. And I like to explain it in my own words. Being in
a party is simple because you're tied to a set of statements the party
defines, and that's it. What we do here is much richer, where we debate, reach agreements, and know whose interests we defend."

Alejandro López thinks none of what lies ahead will be easy.
"The government has a clear agenda of turning natural resources
over to the multinationals and repressing the workers. So, we have
to think about how to involve all of society in every battle of the
struggle. You know, the education problem isn't only the schools'
problem. I have a nine-year-old daughter, so it's my problem too.
The health-care problem isn't the hospitals' problem, it's every-

body's problem; the same with unemployment." Alberto thinks that initiatives like the Alto Valle Coalition (an organization that brings together various movements and unions) can foster the creation of what he calls a *tool.* "We don't want to be the opposition forever—we have to take a step forward. I'm not sure what that step is, but we have to build a forum for discussion, to develop our program, and wage a fight to the finish. We, the workers, are the ones who move the economy. So it's a travesty that the workers don't get to decide what we want for our future."

Alejandro believes that everything can't be based on defending themselves, answering criticisms, and reacting. "We have to go on the offensive. I'm not sure how, but it's precisely something we want to start discussing with our compañeros."

Alberto concludes, "The thing is, if we don't, then they could convince us that the only place where we can make decisions in is the family unit, and not on the societal level. That's horrible. We did something else—we took charge of the means of production and made them work. That, to me, is the most alternative thing there is."

Chapter Two

Brukman
A Struggle That Made History

A small textile factory in the Buenos Aires neighborhood called Once was the protagonist of one of the most passionate, violent, and dramatic chapters of this saga. This is how two of its principal actors remember it.

One day before Argentina exploded with the sound of *cacerolas,* fifty-two seamstresses took a stand before their bosses and demanded their unpaid wages.

Unknowingly, they had only beat that frenetic popular revolt by twenty-four hours, the people yelling, *"Que se vayan todos. Que no quede ni uno solo."* ("They all must go. Every single one must go".) This battle cry did not just refer to the politicians; in this neighborhood it also meant the wealthy businessmen with bankrupt companies and impoverished employees.

Brukman textile company quickly became a symbol of Argentina, post–December 19–20, 2001. It awoke the solidarity of the newborn neighborhood assemblies, as well as the *piquetero* movements, students, and leftist parties. It became the flagship of the reclaimed factories movement, almost like a mecca for activists and researchers. "There is a rumor flying around the world, a rumor that says that there is another way of working, that there is a solution, and the name of that rumor, of that hope, is Brukman," wrote Canadian journalist Naomi Klein.

Brukman possessed several distinctive traits that allowed it to occupy that privileged space. For starters, we are talking about the occupation of a prestigious enterprise with a fifty-year history in the heart of Buenos Aires. On top of that, the majority of the factory's workers were women. Contrary to what tends to happen with women labor leaders, they did not have to hide behind their male comrades in order to express their opinions. Their declarations coincided perfectly with a social context in which women had begun to take a leading role. While middle-class women armed with pots and pans hit the streets to rebel against the state of siege, women from the excluded lower class had already demonstrated their courage by blocking roads and demanding jobs for their families. Up until then, the Brukman workers had identified with neither. Nevertheless, their sky-blue overalls became flags representing the same struggle.

The Brukman struggle was most distinguished by the active participation of leftist parties throughout the course of the occupation. Using their resources and connections, they gave the struggle widespread prominence. While most reclaimed factories or factories in the process of being reclaimed carried on their struggles in silence, Brukman placed itself on the media and political agendas. A minister of then-president Eduardo Duhalde had his secret actions revealed by an associate of the Boca Juniors soccer club, in an interview with lavaca.org. He had hired "The 12" (Boca's *barra brava* or soccer fan club) to create disturbances at the protests after the April 18, 2003, forcible expulsion of the Brukman workers from the plant. The government feared that the Brukman seed would grow into another December 1920. But, on that occasion, the barra brava had to retreat, after a group of piqueteros exposed them.

While the Left turned Brukman into yet another arena for its ongoing confrontations, the movements of reclaimed factories realized that the organized parties' interests did not always coincide with those of the workers themselves. Naomi Klein described it like this on one of her visits: "Something that always caught my attention regarding Brukman before the eviction was that all the leftist parties had come and hung their flags with their logos on the factory front, but no one thought to design a new logo to represent a company run by its workers. That's why there's no sign that reads: Brukman, under worker control."

The Brukman case did not just generate a nasty ideological debate with the sectors that defend the overarching value of private property. It also imposed an internal discussion in the heart of the social movements. Almost from the beginning of the occupation, until achieving the factory's expropriation in October of 2003, there was tension between two currents. On one side, the leftist parties—especially the Workers' Party (PO) and the Socialist Workers Party (PTS)—demanded nationalization of the plant under worker control. On the other side, the adherents to the reclaimed enterprise movement believed there was a faster and more practical solution—expropriation by a worker cooperative. For the former, the cooperatives were puppets within the capitalist system, and not viable due to the lack of capital. They also maintained that the cooperative option only postponed dealing with the root of the problem, because the expropriations granted by the government were temporary, only two years, shadowed by the dubious prospect of a worker buyout of the factory. The defenders of expropriation, on the other hand, were pragmatic—if they formed the cooperative, the seamstresses would recover their source of income, which was the initial objective of most of the workers.

These two different visions had, in Brukman, two spokeswomen.

On one side, Celia Martínez.

On the other, Matilde Adorno.

Their pointed discussions became classics at the assemblies.

Here they narrate their story.

Through their memories, passions, and sacrifices, we get a sense of the struggle that made history—the Battle of Brukman.

"We Learned to Have Ideals"
Interview with Matilde Adorno

Do you remember how the occupation of the factory was organized?

It happened naturally. We were going on fifteen days during which, although there was a ton of work, they didn't pay us a cent. There was growing unrest that broke out on the fifth floor, in the pants section, where there was a smaller group than ours—we're from the coat section, the largest. Their anger was boiling over faster than ours, and they practically stopped production. It was

peak season and they had to turn out 3,500 pants—shorts, actually. The manager coerced people, told them that if they didn't
work, they wouldn't get paid at all. Supposedly we took home a
hundred pesos every Friday, but that was already history at that
point. They would give us ten, fifteen, five, even as little as two
pesos. Even so, they kept the pressure on. That's when the pants
section just stopped production, so that they would give us some
money. But they never thought about taking over the factory.

But they took it…

That last Friday they gave us two pesos and told us not to show up
the whole next week. We said no, we'll be here on Tuesday for
them to give us something. To make matters worse, they had already made us sign stating that we would take unpaid leave. We
were terrified—there was work, they wouldn't pay us, they told us
not to come in, and they had even made us sign for unpaid leave.
That Tuesday we sat at our workstations and, at 7 a.m., when the
executives showed up, we came downstairs en masse to see how
much money they were going to give us. An argument broke out
and Jacobo Brukman came out and said, "Okay, if you think you
manage the factory better than us, here, take the key." But he put
it back in his pocket. And Enrique Brukman said, "Who do you
think you are, that I'm going to bring the money from abroad to
pay you." He closed the door and left. The manager told us to go
back to work and to come back downstairs later to see how much
money he could come up with. When we went down, they had all
left—there were only a couple of salespeople on the first floor. At
3 p.m. they hadn't come back. At four they still hadn't come. At

7:30 I said, "Well, I can't stay any longer." I had a previous engage-
ment. But the idea to stay until they came back with the money
was already on the table. Honestly, we never thought that they
wouldn't come back. Twenty-three people stayed. Those of us who
left never imagined that they would stay overnight.

*And what did you think when you went back to the factory the fol-
lowing day?*

I saw people in the street, a police car. I thought it was all over.
When I saw the signs I almost dropped dead.... Inside I found
everyone looking pretty scared. The night watchman had left at 5
a.m. and left the key with those who stayed, who locked themselves in until we got there. They had decided that the workers
could go in, but the managers didn't want to go in until the owners got there, because they were more like the boss than the boss
himself—more Catholic than the Pope. It still hadn't occurred to
us that they weren't going to come. As the day wore on and they
didn't show up—all day we waited and no one came—we just
wanted to die, we were desperate. We spent the first day waiting
for them to come, staring at the walls.

Meanwhile, the country exploded. That day was December 19, 2001...

We were so absorbed by our own situation, getting paid two pesos
to get home and get back to work, that we didn't even know there
was another reality. All we knew about the piqueteros was that they
would block roads and make us late for work. I remember how that
night most of the workers stayed. The only ones who didn't go inside at all were the salespeople, the three executives, and the office

errand boy. When he showed up the next day we let him have it. Since the front of the building is all glass, the security guard showed us where to put up a cardboard screen so you couldn't see in from the outside. One coworker sat at a desk and most of the rest laid down on the floor. That night a lawyer called and told us a state of siege had been declared. He told us that we should take down all the signs we had put up—that said "We want to get paid"—and stay inside. We were scared to death. Some co-workers, especially the men, began to leave, until Juanita stood up and said, "No, no one else is leaving this place. This belongs to everyone." She stood in front of the door, grabbed the key, and put it right here (*she gestures to her bra*) and said again, "Nobody moves."

And what happened when you heard the cacerolazos?

At some point during the night we began to hear noises and someone said, "It's the *gendarmería* (Federal Police) coming to kick us out." And when we took a peek outside, it was people banging pots and pans. We didn't understand at all. We didn't have a TV or a radio. Actually, there were some TVs in the offices, but we had locked them up because we didn't want to touch anything, so they couldn't blame us for anything. Always thinking that the owners would show up at any moment. There we stood, tense, frightened … That's how the 19th and the 20th were. I even remember Juanita saying, "That state of siege thing is for the people causing disturbances, it's not because of us." When de la Rúa resigned, we were eating a rice stew that we had made with what neighboring stores had given us. We were so terrified…. The mistake was theirs, the owners—because if they had come, even three days later, with ten pesos, we would have grabbed those ten pesos and left. I remember that a couple of days later some folks from Telefónica [one of the telephone companies] came by. They asked what was going on with us and we told them. They said, "You can't stay in here—how will anyone find out what's happening to you? You have to go outside, pitch a tent, ask for donations for a strike fund, block the street..." We said they were crazy. We couldn't bring ourselves to do that. We also went to the Ministry of Labor and found out that the union had declared bankruptcy—precisely what we didn't want. They wanted bankruptcy to get paid what the company owed them, but that's not what we wanted.

What is it that you wanted?

To get paid, that's all. Bankruptcy, no way. We wanted to continue working—the only thing we wanted was to get paid. We were ready to kill the union because they said they couldn't come since they had a lot of things to do. They never showed their faces while—as we later came to realize—we were occupying the factory. That's why we kicked the union rep out on her rear end. After that, many other women that were with the rep left with her. Meanwhile, we're still thinking, "Well, it'll be a week, two weeks..." It already seemed like an eternity and now that it's been two years, I can't believe it.

You never heard back from the company?

At one point the manager showed up at the bar on the corner. He called us and said he wanted to negotiate. Some coworkers went and the guy said, "Okay guys, take three or four suits each—I'll

give you fifty pesos, just leave. We'll go in later and fix things up."
We said no and protested by blockading the street the following
day. It was something we hadn't thought through at all, that,
thank God, turned out well. One time a journalist asked us if we
had the possibility of choosing between the time when everything
was normal and we worked and got paid on time, and this, the
time of struggle, which would we choose? What a stupid question,
I thought then. The first choice, I replied. Most of us are older
women, almost ready for retirement, and struggle is fine and all—
the class struggle, as we've since learned—but we're not fit to be
fighting in the street all the time, when we could be working. Of
course we can support all those who are struggling. We learned to
have ideals—we learned that everyone deserves what they earn.
We were really exploited in there, especially toward the end.

*Did the successive government changes affect the workers' spirits or de-
cisions?*

No. We were terrified. We had gotten into something that we didn't
understand. Luckily, it went OK. Only some, who joined one political party or another, began to understand things, and came and
went with advice. Of course, most of the time, they did this secretly.
Only the most perceptive figured it out. Finally, when we were out
on the street, after the last expulsion, everyone realized. Really, the
only thing the majority had done until then was work, work, and
work. They didn't see any further. If we had to go somewhere, they
would say, "Yeah, he can go, I'll stay." They didn't worry about there
being different visions. The only thing they cared about was for
there to be some money to take home on Friday.

The political parties approached you soon after?

When we took the factory, people would talk to me about the "Left" and, to me, it was a single party. I had no idea that there were so many. For me, there was one and that's it. When I saw that there was one here, another over there, they pulled this way, and that way, they talked your ear off ... I just wanted to shoot myself. But, yes, they came around about that time. Actually, the first ones that came were from the IMPA (a worker cooperative association), to see if we wanted to form a cooperative. But we still thought that the owners would be here any minute, and we would negotiate. We started working, but I think it wasn't until we pitched the tent outside that we realized that they weren't coming back.

That was the spring when the idea to form a cooperative came up?

Yes. The legislature later told us that we had to form a cooperative because they couldn't turn the factory over to just any John or Jane Doe. Some of the political groups didn't want to—they told us that things were going badly for other cooperatives. I went to talk to the people at Lavalán and that turned out to be a lie. There were two or three of us who fought over this—the majority wasn't paying attention to what was being discussed—they didn't get it. The majority just waited for Friday, hoping to take some money home with them.

Was it a pragmatic or ideological discussion?

It was ideological. The parties that weren't in favor of the coopera-tives said we would turn into new bosses. But if we're going to be a worker cooperative and we all earn the same amount, and if we're going to decide everything by assembly, where is the boss? Here it's not going to be like in other reclaimed factories where they have managers that make a bit more money. We don't agree with that.

When did you take over the factory and prepare to work under self-management?

More than anything, it was when the Port Said company urgently needed us to turn in those shorts, because it was peak season. We decided to deliver the merchandise and they paid us. With that money we ran and paid Edesur so they wouldn't cut off the electricity. We reached a deal with them, that we would pay the bills from the time of our occupying the factory on. Everything before that was not our debt. We paid the electricity, gas, telephone, and what was left we distributed amongst ourselves in equal shares. At that time there were a lot more of us, we were all still there. Later, when the money ran out, a lot of people left. There are people—I understand them—that had to support a household. They couldn't make ends meet on a dream. Our dream came true, but it was a very, very tough fight. There were people who had to pay the rent, and I understand that. I understand my coworkers who left.

Some of your coworkers call those who left "scabs" and don't think allowing them to return, as the Expropriation Law dictates, is fair.

That's no good. I fight against that—a scab is someone who breaks a strike. They left because they thought—just like we who stayed thought—that the owners would come back any minute. They bet on that. At that time, who would have thought that we would end up keeping the factory? Not even we did … We called and talked to them several times. We explained that our job was not just to work, that we had to fight, that it meant going to one event, and then maybe another. They couldn't accept it. They wanted to show up, put in their working hours, and leave. They didn't want to take responsibility for the struggle that lay ahead of us. It's just that no one thought it was going to be such a long and tedious struggle. Most of us thought it would be a month—but then it was another month, then one more—but never two years. It was the same thing after the last time they evicted us. We never thought we would spend six months in a tent. I remember when someone came from one of the parties and said we were going to be there three months. We all said, "What? No way!" We told him to hit the road. Then we spent six months there.

What did you decide to do after selling all the merchandise to Port Said?

Well…we were left with nothing. We held an assembly to see what we would do. We decided to open the plant and start working. That was in mid-January.

Everyone agreed to go back to work?

I wasn't at that assembly, but we always held that when there is a majority decision in an assembly, we all act accordingly.

How did you organize yourselves to initiate production?

At first it was chaotic because the production line wasn't complete. So we all had to learn to do all sorts of things. Also, none of the administration people were left. The Engineering School invited us to a meeting of reclaimed factories that helped us a lot with that problem. Some of us went to the meeting and they asked us what we needed, and we asked for people to help us with the administration. That's how an economist showed up, and stuck with us until the very last day. The meeting also inspired us to go out and sell our products. Together with Oscar, a compañero, they walked all over Buenos Aires. They found us clients who keep us in business to this very day. We started to sell—enough to pay what we needed to pay—the electricity, the gas, the telephone. We even cut back on some costs, to spend less, like not using gas on some floors.

Did you always distribute earnings equally?

Always. At no point did anyone oppose this. And now we're going to continue this way. If there are ten pesos, we distribute them among everyone, after setting aside what we need to pay the bills. We had to buy all the raw materials. We also did a lot of custom work, *à façon*. The client provides us the material or advances us the money to buy it. Last summer, when there were no materials, the college student who came to help us said, "Don't take any money home right now; buy fabric." We did as he said and bought a ton. Because of that we had a fantastic summer. We're here today because of that fabric.

What was it like the first time you were kicked out of the building, in March of 2002?

That eviction was somewhat violent, though not nearly as much as the one in November. Judge Velazco ordered us out in March, but then said that since it was a labor, not legal conflict, we had the right to be in the factory. But later, on November 23, they tossed us out again. It was unbelievable, done by the GEO[1] swat team. I was alone on the third floor, on a mattress next to a sewing machine. When I opened my eyes, I saw a guy in a ski mask pointing an Itaka shotgun at my head. I thought I was in a movie—I couldn't believe this was happening. They came in by breaking all the doors down using their rifle butts—it was pretty dramatic. They didn't believe me that I was there alone. There was another coworker on the sixth floor, and another on the first floor, with her nine-year-old daughter, who was also arrested. Walking out of the factory, it was like a militarized zone, full of soldiers—incredible. That's when they charged us with trespassing and theft, and issued a fine for 50,000 pesos.

Where did they take you?

They took us down to the first floor, where there were doctors who wanted to examine us. I told them not to touch me—no way—I didn't want anything to do with them. The owners were standing in the doorway. That same day they took us to a police station on the total opposite side of the city. One by one they escorted us away—normal cops in unmarked cars. While I was in the car I was mentally saying good-bye to everything—it was all so violent—I thought we would never go back inside [the factory] again. I thought they would take us to a local police station, but the car kept going, and going, and I asked them where they were taking me. I ended up near General Paz[2], because that's where the charges had been made. I even got to the point of thinking "I am just going to be one more missing person." Who would know about me? The police took us away at twenty minutes to seven in the morning and they found us at twelve thirty in the afternoon.

How did you reenter the factory that time?

We were detained in a place where we couldn't see or call anyone. I said to the police, "How is this possible…is it only in the movies that you're allowed to make one phone call?" I had my cell phone and they didn't even let me touch it. Then, when the lawyer got there, they transferred us to some offices that had televisions. And that's when we saw that we were back in the factory. Our coworkers had been pushing up against the police barricades around the factory, and they later told us that the policemen themselves were telling them, "Push harder so we can go home soon." When we went back there was a whole celebration to welcome us back…they reluctantly gave me my mattress back.

By that time you were no longer demanding the factory be national-
ized—how did things change?

The nationalization idea came from a party, not our assembly. Later on when they explained it to us, we said that would be fabulous, but not with the current government. At some point, perhaps, but not until after a serious revolution. I can just see this government nationalizing this small factory! I would ask the people in favor of nationalization, "Do you want Ibarra[3] to be our boss?" It drove me nuts. If this were nationalized, we would get paid, but Ibarra would be our boss. There was talk of Ibarra this and Ibarra that.

Many groups approached Brukman offering solidarity—political par-
ties, assemblies, cultural groups, journalists. What was that like?

At some points it caused a lot of anger and confrontations, because most of us were against so many people showing up—all that coming and going of people we didn't know. It caused rifts between us, because there were those who were in favor and those not in favor. It was very hard—we were so many different things. There were many grassroots folks who came to collaborate with us, but there were more who wanted to pull us in some direction. We are ready to listen to what they tell us, think it over, and we'll see—but none of this wanting to take us to be part of one party or another party. Ninety-five percent of [the Brukman workers] are independents. Just because we listen to one or another [party or group] doesn't mean that we belong to it.

At what point in the whole process did you feel the most torn?

In mid-2002. All kinds of terrible things were going on, lots of anger. We would hear coworkers say that they didn't belong to any party and then we would see them at one party's headquarters all the time. And their way of defending themselves was to accuse you of belonging to another party. The months we spent outside the factory served us well to reflect and see all these things. Now we're much stricter with the parties. While still inside the factory we had already decided to kick all the parties out. Let them be present, but outside. Because you would turn around, and there one was. There was no privacy among the workers. They came and went, eavesdropping on everything. Now and then they would cause a big uproar, because one person would defend these guys, someone else would defend the others.... The media was also everywhere—you would be working and they would stick a camera in your face. We couldn't work like that. They would show up and come on in whenever they wanted. And sometimes whoever was guarding the door would let whomever

they wanted come in. One of the bigger incidents we had was when
we were in the tent,[4] when the people listening in from outside the
tent got into physical fight over what we were debating inside.

What happened?

Well…the parties. We weren't in agreement with one of our
coworkers running in the elections as a "Brukman worker."[5] We
weren't against her running personally, but when she appeared in
all the posters in her overalls as a Brukman worker, it was terrible.
We just wanted to die. On top of it, there was the constant denial
by certain people that she would run, and then we had to find out
at the last minute.

*Did relations between the workers deteriorate much after living to-
gether so long and so much discussion?*

I think we know each other a lot better. When the owners were
here you would come in at six in the morning and leave at three in
the afternoon, but you didn't really bond. We could talk very little
among ourselves. When we started to spend twenty-four hours a
day with each other, it was awful, until you get used to it and realize who is who. It was hard for many of us to get along—you have
to treat everyone as an individual. Now we know how everyone
else eats, sleeps, and breathes, so we're at peace. At the assemblies
we can be tearing each other apart defending our respective points
of view, but then afterwards we share some *mate*.

You also disciplined each other…

What happens is that there are coworkers who don't get used to
the fact that we have to get all the work done, together. So if one

asks another to do a job, he/she gets scolded, "Who are you, the boss?" We all have to be working as a team. The internal friction motivated us to set up punishments. We punished three workers for disrespecting other workers. One time was because a coworker brought another's dirty laundry out in the open and made her cry. It was atrocious. If people are stressed out, you need to be careful. There needs to be some respect.

We still haven't talked about the last time you were kicked out of the factory ...

We had a ton of work that day, around 400 suits to turn in. It was Holy Thursday, so we decided to take off until Monday. Four coworkers stayed the night, on a rotating watch. They came to kick us out at midnight. I had left late. When I left I had a strange feeling in my gut. I thought, "So many days away from the factory." I'm Catholic, so I went to mass. When I got home at almost midnight, my stomach was still in knots. That's when Zenón, who was at the factory, called and told me, "Matilde, they're kicking us out." It was raining. I was in pajamas. I started making calls to see who could go with me. I went with my brother, and when I got there and saw such a big police operation, I thought that this time would surely be the last.

What were the following days like, with all the protests and the discussions about retaking the factory?

I think we could have retaken the factory on Good Friday. There were a lot of people around. The judge was at the police station and there were lots of government people, who still ask us what we did that day. Our lawyers were also there, fighting to get the police

withdrawn. While the people applied pressure, everyone was
there...so that the judge would concede. But at one point the
judge asked to be left alone. Then he came out again, and ruled in
our favor. Then it seems a compañero told the protesters they
could go home.

Why did they tell everyone to leave?

No one can explain it, though it's been discussed plenty. I have my
theory, but I'm not going to talk about it. When we went to talk
with the government about the expropriation, they were still asking us what happened, why we let all the people go when the
judge was about to sign the agreement. It's an issue that no one
can clarify.

Then came the day when you fought the police to reenter the building.
How was the decision to go in made?

Actually, it was because of pressure from below. I was one of the
ones who knocked down the police fence, but I had always said it
was a crazy idea to go in that way. If it did come to pass, I thought,
I would climb a tree and watch it from above. I was with all the
workers at the front, and behind us were the people from Zanón. I
remember they were putting lime on their faces and I told them,
"You make me laugh, we're up at the front and we don't have anything..." They told me I had to put some on and I made fun of
them—I told them it would make my makeup run. I never
thought I would be doing that. In a situation with so many people
and so much tension, if you want to go in, you tell the others to
go for it, "OK, now." It was very impulsive. It was never discussed
at the assembly, for example.

What was the moment when you knocked down the fence like?

The government was negotiating—they would ask us for ten more minutes, five more minutes.... And when we realized what was going on, we were already inside. We walked in singing, the four of us, arm in arm. At the time I didn't realize there were four of us linked—I found out when I saw the videos. Until then, I had thought it was just Celia and me. I walked in singing, looking at the police, to see their reaction. When we saw that they had started shooting, we ran toward a wall. We saw the bullets flying and couldn't believe it. They advanced and plowed everything over, leaving us behind—we didn't even feel the gas. Then they turned around and told us, "Okay, now get out." I ran out. It was funny to me how the compañeros who said they would take care of us ended up stampeding us. I ran and ran and passed by my car along the way, but there was no way I was going to stop and get in. When I managed to stop I saw a man who was very winded and couldn't speak. I asked him if he would go with me to find my car, because I was scared to go back alone. "Sure compañera, let's go," he said. After getting in the car with him and putting it in gear, I realized he was Representative Roselli.[6] I knew that in the next few days we had to go to Congress to meet with a representative, but not that the meeting was with the very man whom I was talking with.

What assessment did you make in the following assemblies?

I don't know. I was somewhat dazed. We said we had wanted to do something, but not *that*. It was like it had been a trap. Why did we do it? The pressure finally made us go in. We thought they wouldn't repel us, wouldn't touch us. That's why they made us, the women, go up front. At one point we felt used. Many activists from the assemblies told us they had come to support us with their kids, and they had already been questioning us before we went in.

How was the decision to pitch the tent made?

After the repression we organized a huge march, then pitched the tent out on Belgrano (an important nearby avenue), until we moved it in front of the factory. We all agreed we couldn't leave. The PTS comrades brought us the tent, and we later paid them back for it. It's ours—it cost us 300 pesos.

What changed once you were outside?

My coworkers became more politically conscious, more than during the entire year and a half inside. They came to understand what struggle is about, they learned to not let themselves be fooled, to not keep quiet. They learned that they have to defend their own ideas.

There was a time that the encampment seemed to be losing momentum, that the workers seemed to be very alone. How did that climate affect you?

I caught bronchitis, which I still can't shake. Everyone had to battle depression, fatigue, the thought that there was no solution. Many wanted to go out and look for work. Because a strike fund can give you ten pesos, but not enough to pay a bill, or much of anything.

Did you never think of looking for another job?

I was offered another job, but that would have meant abandoning the struggle. It was a choice. Many of us chose to stay.

What had changed? A while ago you told me that if you had the

choice, you would have gone back to the old days of a job with super-
visors and a boss.

Do you know how many times I told myself that today was the *last*
day I would go to the tent? Days when I thought I would never get
out of bed—and I would get up. If we had reached that point, how
could I give up then? Each person has her story. Maybe I stayed because I have my daughter who sends some money my way. But others
don't have anything, and they were forced to go out and find work.

How much money did you each make while you were working?

The most we took home was 100 pesos a week.

And while you were outside the factory, how did you get by?

With the strike funds. A lot was donated from abroad, from Ger-
many, from France, from England. We received an order from
England for some handkerchiefs at spectacular prices—US$1.70.[7]
And for doing a simple hem, nothing more.

What did your families think about the conflict?

We have a coworker who got separated—her husband left her.
And many husbands were skeptical, until we realized that we
could tell the husbands, children, siblings to come with us....
That's when everything calmed down.

Were there also love stories?

Oh, any number of them. I think three babies were born during
that time.

"Now I See Everything Through Different Eyes"
Interview with Celia Martínez

Do you remember how you decided to take over the factory?

There was no decision made to occupy the factory—there was a decision to stay and wait for the owner to bring the money to pay us. I left late that night, but other coworkers who didn't even have money for the bus home, stayed. It wasn't thought through at all.

You never thought you would take the factory?

Never. I hoped the boss would come back, I pleaded for him to come back. I even spoke on the phone with Jaime Muscat—the Brukmans' lawyer, who in the end confronted us—for him to help us, to see what we could do. A week before the events of the 18th, the doorman had told me that the management had been removing things from the factory at night, as if to provoke us to do something. I called Muscat because he was the lawyer who had left the company some time before—we were sad when he left—he seemed to have good intentions to help the factory. And what do you know, we were talking with our mortal enemy. But I insist—we hadn't the slightest intention of taking over a factory.

And what happened the next day?

On December 18th I left at 11 p.m. and my coworkers stayed. That night they held an assembly and decided to ask the doorman for the key and take charge until the owner returned to pay us. I came back at five in the morning. They came to the door and said, "If you're going to stay and fight, come in. If not, don't." Most of the people who stayed out were foremen, supervisors, office people, runners, and the human resources manager.... The workers, we went in.

Why do you think they didn't go in?

They thought we were doing something illegal. We thought so too.

Were you scared?

No, no. The previous night the police had stopped by and asked us to tell them if we needed any help, and if anything happened to let them know.

What were the discussions about at that time?

We thought the police would come, that we shouldn't touch anything. I mean, all the doors were open, including the manager's office—of course we thought they would come back. I was in charge of locking all the doors so no one would touch anything, to see if anything was missing.... We never thought we would end up in charge of the factory. At night, a co-worker who was part of a group called Techo y Trabajo (Roof and Work) that fights for affordable housing, called her organization and said we needed food. We had nothing—not even tea and sugar for *mate*. The people came and brought us a bunch of food; we pulled it up using a rope. They filled our whole table—two and a half meters long—and we started to ask ourselves what we would do with so much food. That night was December 19th and we hung a banner out the window saying "Cavallo must go."

It was December 19, 2001. Did you know what was going on outside?

One of our coworkers, Juan Carlos, really likes music, so he's always listening to the radio. That's how we found out that the government had declared a state of siege and we thought, "*Mamita*, now the government is going to come kick us out and give us a beating." We closed everything, locked the door and went to the very back of the plant without making a sound. One of us sat at the reception desk, as if she were a secretary. At night, when we heard the cacerolazos, we thought it was the gendarmería coming to get us.

Were you aware of the magnitude of what was going on, or did you remain absorbed in your own conflict?

Look, on the 20th there was a reconciliation meeting at the Labor Ministry. We wanted the owners to come back, but with money. We didn't want two pesos anymore, we were asking for at least fifty or a hundred. That was all we demanded. We spoke with the union delegate, who was still inside the factory, and she communicated with the union. That's how they let us know about the negotiations. I called my personal lawyer to have him accompany us, because we didn't have one. At the hearing, neither the bosses nor their lawyers appeared. No one went to represent the company. The hearing was dismissed and they were just at that moment evacuating the Ministry because there was a tremendous mess brewing outside. The troops had already reached Callao[8] and people were running. We walked out and saw Coca-Cola bottles flying. We got scared—seriously scared! We started to run and, on top of all that, I was running after the union delegate because I wanted a copy of the statement that had been signed. I couldn't find her anywhere. Just then I turned around and saw a police

horse stomping on a journalist's chest. What terror! I cried as I
ran—I felt totally abandoned. Our group had run every which
way—it was chaos. Everyone had left and I don't know the city
very well, because I'm from Claypole (in Greater Buenos Aires). I
still don't know the streets, which is why I take taxis most of the
time. I asked myself, "What do I do? Where do I go?" I ran and
ran until I got into a taxi.... I didn't know it, but I was two blocks
from the factory by then. I was really upset because I couldn't find
anybody. It turns out I had reached Brukman before the rest.

How did the leftist parties approach the Brukman workers?

Already on the 20th people from the Workers' Party were stopping
by the factory. I would come to the door to talk with them, but always with the door closed. They talked about strange things, told
us we had to stay, that we should take the factory. I thought they
were all communists. I would call home and tell my husband,
"We're surrounded by communists."

What was the Left to you?

Nothing—I had no idea. I come from Claypole, where the whole
neighborhood is Peronist. All our friends are part of the local PJ[9]
delegation. My husband and I always voted, we would go to the
headquarters, the local PJ office. But we never participated actively
in politics. We would discuss, like, "We need to vote for Menem,
because of this, for Duhalde because of that." We were with
Cafiero[10] because he came to the neighborhood, to the local office.
We always voted Peronist.

How did your opinion change?

Every day university students would come by. I would listen to them from behind the bars and answer yes or no, nothing more. Until Carlitos Brown, a kid from Contraimagen (an alternative media organization), from the University's School of Philosophy, showed up. He had this crazy look about him... he started telling us how there was an occupied factory in Neuquén—he was talking about Zanón. He told us that we had to stay in Brukman and put it back to work. He talked to us about politics, what happened in Russia, and this and that.... Always from the other side of the bars. Then came people from Polo Obrero.[11] Since they were older, we gave them more credit. They went with us to do paperwork at the Labor Sub-secretariat. A professor from the Mariano Acosta School also came by—we later found out he was with Polo Obrero. Then came the PTS. I didn't want anything to do with Polo Obrero—the PTS, even less. They all came and went because they saw the little banner that said "Cavallo must go." We later changed it for another that said, "Occupied factory." They would tell us we needed to block the street so people would realize that the shameless owner hadn't paid us. So finally we did our first roadblock on December 27th and 28th—because on the 24th there had been another special hearing at the Labor Ministry and the owners hadn't shown up again. They pulled the same thing again on the 26th. The union told us there was nothing we could do, because the company was bankrupt. "We asked them to declare bankruptcy," the union told us. Instinctively, I told them, "You're supposed to defend us—to fight for them to pay us and keep our jobs. What do you mean you told them to declare bankruptcy?" They answered that they did it because the company owed them a lot of money. I went nuts and started insulting them. When I went back to the factory I told the union delegate that she was a disgrace....

No one had spoken of expropriation until then?

No, no. It was only finally in January that people from the INAES[12] came and talked to us about the cooperatives. Then came Murúa,[13] of the Reclaimed Factories Movement, and told us that we could form one. We were about to do it, but we changed our minds.

Why?

We received more up-to-date news about how Zanón was doing. We knew what they were demanding. They sent us letters showing their solidarity. A kid from En Clave Roja[14] had approached us on behalf of the University's School of Economics, who proposed that we try a project to supply materials to the city. We studied it, talked it over in the assembly and we thought it was a good idea. I remember that I read it aloud in the assembly and we voted on it. So we decided not to form the cooperative. After that, the long negotiations with the Labor Ministry began, where they wanted to give us a Plan Trabajar.[15] We rejected it—we considered ourselves employed workers.

At that point you still wanted to reach an agreement with the owner, right?

I think so. Until about January 15th, when we restarted production in the factory, we were waiting for them to come. If they would have come and reopened the plant, everything would have been fine.

Why did you decide to restart production yourselves?

Because at the Labor Secretariat we told them that we had no money—that we needed to do *something*. We mentioned how customers would come by every day, and that if the factory were open, we could sell clothes. We didn't want to touch anything— the doors to the stockroom were sacred. One day, some of the workers tried to open them and I, who had locked the doors, threatened to report them to the police for theft. See how I used to be! But at the same time the Secretariat told us that we could sell the clothes because we had made them, and it would be a way of paying ourselves the wages owed us. We thought this was good; we went back to Brukman and informed our coworkers. By then, we had already formed an internal commission of six members, and I was one of them. That day we decided to open the stockroom. And that's when the issue of the Left parties really began. We had already begun to trust that kid from Contraimagen, Carlitos Brown, even though he seemed crazy, and we let him come inside. He told us how, in other eras, factories had been placed under worker control. He's from the PTS, and he would tell us about times long ago, about Marx, Trotsky. We didn't get it, but I started to listen. I liked to listen, to learn, and I started to get hooked. And whatever I become convinced of, I try to convince others too.

So that's how your conversion from Peronist to Trotskyist happened?

It was almost unintentional and against my will. Yuri, another coworker, talked about strange things, but he had been active in a leftist party in Bolivia. Elisa and Carlos were also active in other parties. To me, they were the communists. I didn't trust them one bit. A psychology student who is now in Spain had also come by. I never knew what party he was from, but we talked a lot and they gradually convinced me.

And how did things go once you started selling products?

Since we sold everything so quickly, we decided to start producing to restock. There was also an order from the Port Said company. We said, "Okay, we'll produce as long as it sells." We had some sense of security because they had told us at the Ministry that we could do it, even though they had said it in that "you didn't hear it from us" tone. In any case, we still kept people on guard at night. In February we reached another reconciliation at the Ministry, with Minister Atanasoff and the owners. It took about eight hours. I remember we still said that the factory was at the owner's disposition, but that he had to pay us everything he owed us. The Brukmans' proposal was to close the factory for three months, give us some suits, and keep paying us, little by little, with whatever sales revenue came in. So if they sold a single suit, they would divide the money among the 115 workers. Because the deal was with everyone—not just with the fifty-two of us who were inside. Of course we rejected the offer.

And how did you organize the work?

Everyone knew what to do; each person took his or her place to do respective tasks. We named a coordinator for each sector and chose some of our coworkers to work on sales. The internal commission took care of public relations and went to the negotiations, then came and brought everything to the assembly. Then lawyers from the CEPRODH[16] came. They offered to support us and we accepted because we didn't have any other legal help. Since my personal lawyer advised us to accept the owners' proposal, we told him we preferred to take a different route.

Were there problems over who did or didn't do their job?

Not many, but there was some friction here and there. As time went on the accusations came out, "What are you doing?" "You're slacking off," and so on. It continues today.

And how do you resolve that kind of problem?

Now we're organized by sector, and each sector commits to complete a determined amount of production, and has to do it. And when it doesn't work, we get angry. What are we going to do? Kill our coworker? Sometimes there are technical problems, or sometimes people work faster and finish their jobs early, and then others look at them resentfully because they're just standing around.

And how do you distribute earnings?

The treasurer we elected holds on to the revenues. We always distribute them in equal parts, leaving a fund to buy supplies and pay the bills. We had to negotiate with Edesur, and also with the gas company. They let us pay the owners' debt in installments. In those days we were taking about 100 pesos home a week. The time we paid ourselves the most was the week before the kids went back to school. Our coworkers' kids hadn't had new shoes, overalls, or school supplies in a long time. So we distributed everything there was, about 500 pesos each.

When did you start demanding nationalization?

In February we presented a proposal to the Legislature.

Why did the nationalization option interest you?

The government puts huge contracts up for bids from its suppliers. Those guys that work with the government—how much money do they make for approving this or that contract? We wanted Brukman's products to go straight to the hospitals, to the government's distribution centers, without intermediaries. For us, it was also a way of securing our salaries.

Didn't it imply overly believing in a state that had shown its incapability to meet its citizens' basic needs?

But after the 19th and 20th, I thought everything had changed, because people had changed. I myself see everything with different eyes. I think we need to fight.

What changed within yourself?

I don't just go home after work anymore, to do laundry, iron, and cook. I study Marxism, I go to the lectures at cultural centers, feminist meetings with Pan y Rosas. Now I'm interested in everything.

Was it unanimous to nationalize the factory?

When I am convinced of something, I stand up at the assembly and say it. There were many discussions after the eviction where I was blamed for our ending up outside the factory. Obviously, if I'm convinced of something I want to try and convince them—but I can't take responsibility for what the group voted for or decided. No one put a gun to their heads to vote against forming a cooperative, to fight for the factory's nationalization, to go to a march, to block the street, or to organize a festival. If I have to sell you a suit, I try to convince you. Maybe it's missing a leg, but if you buy it, you can't make me responsible for a decision you made of your own will.

Didn't the possibility of becoming an owner of your own factory though the Expropriation Law[17] interest you?

In two years, at our current pace, we won't be able to buy the factory. Why should we deceive ourselves, if we can't produce enough to make a profit, save up, and buy the plant?

There are factories that have done it …

But it depends on the industry they're in. It depends on many things. Jacobo Brukman is going around saying, "It doesn't matter what these riff-raff do, in any case, in two years they'll be on the street and I'll be back in the factory." They're the owners. Of course we shouldn't feel inferior to them, but we already have a 50,000-peso debt with the Banco Ciudad that we used to buy supplies. It's fine that we have a one-year grace period to pay it, but in a capitalist state like this one it's really hard.

How much money are you taking home right now?

About 100 or 150 a week.

Throughout the conflict you were approached by students, groups, political parties. Did you feel at any point that you were being pressured and that the workers stopped making strategic decisions?

No, everything was always decided by assembly, for better or for worse, right or wrong. When some of my coworkers say, when they are angry, that we spent so much time stuck in conflict because of the PTS, or because of me, I always say that if I convinced them, it's been because I must have a gift for it. A gift that perhaps Luis Caro, of the Movement of Reclaimed Factories, has now. I still think that what I did was right.

You don't have anything to criticize yourself about?

There are things we may not have done well. Perhaps we should have accepted the idea of creating a cooperative some time earlier. In October of 2003 we had already presented a proposal in which we asked for the expropriation of the factory, the brands, the machines, and licenses. On top of it, we were explicit about being open to any kind of legal form so long as the factory was given to the workers. But the government said no to everything. We had stepped back from demanding nationalization, but they said they no longer approved anything, that too much time had passed. Perhaps we should have taken that road before April 18th, when they kicked us out. What we weren't watching closely enough is how they had already tried to kick the workers out at Zanón. We were so absorbed in our work that we didn't pay attention to that.

What do you remember about that confrontation over Easter?

I was on the bus at 11 p.m. on a route that went about three blocks from the factory. I had been at the University Social Sciences department, where it was decided that I would be one of the

PTS candidates for the National House of Representatives. I didn't see anything out of the ordinary. When I got home, I started to change and they called me to tell me. I got dressed again, ran out, caught a cab, and was at Brukman by one.

The following Friday it seemed that you were about to get back in, but it all ended in nothing. What happened?

The municipal government had said it would guarantee our reentry if the judge turned the factory over to us, but the agreement wasn't accepted. Even Hebe de Bonafini[18] had come by that day. There was tremendous pressure—the people wanted to go in. We said no, that we wanted to do things right, legally. I had seen some kids from Venceremos[19] who were up front, all riled up. They wanted to cause trouble at all costs…they were throwing rocks at the police. I told them not to, that they were going to get killed. At that time we asked the people gathered to disperse, because I was really afraid the police were going to shoot at them. Many people said that it was the PTS's fault that we didn't go in, because we called off the crowd. But even the PTS came to ask me why Yuri and I came out and said that we were negotiating. It's just that we couldn't imagine those kids, so young, dead.

And what changed by the following Monday for you to knock down the police fence and try to get in?

That day we were negotiating with the National Ombudswoman, Nana Bevilaqua. We asked Chiche Duhalde,[20] who was campaigning at the time, to please come, as a compañera, to help us. We also spoke with the Labor Minister, Graciela Caamaño. I was explaining to her that under no circumstances would we abandon our positions on the police lines. At one point the girls told me, "Let's go in, let's go in." I told them to wait, that we were negotiating with the minister. But then there was nothing left to discuss. The Chief of Police told us that we couldn't go in, not even to negotiate. That made us feel so angry—impotent. I was under a lot of pressure; all the workers from the factory were right behind me, because we had said that if someone was going to go down, we would be the first. I was holding on to the fence and Juanita, Estela, and Delia Figueroa were yelling to me, "Let's go in, let's go in, let's go in!" I turned around and snapped at them, asking if they *really* wanted to go in. When they answered yes, I turned back around and pushed the fence. I latched on to three compañeras who had stepped forward and we moved ahead. It was a moment of anger—a lightning bolt. When the fence fell I saw the police lift their rifles and take aim. Then they started shooting. I thought, "They're going to kill us, right here." We all ran together into a corner and huddled in front of the neighboring laboratory. I couldn't stop thinking that we were so close and still not quite there. People were running everywhere. All of a sudden I remembered that my two daughters were there. The idea that I had lost them terrified me.

Was the decision to go in sincere?

I don't know. It wasn't thought through. I never took into account that the Madres were up front, or my eighteen-year-old daughter, who ended up fainting ...

How did you decide to pitch a tent?

The PTS proposed it. We were in front of the fence, with the idea of staying there, regardless of the elements. When they asked, we said okay. I thought they would bring small camping tents. Suddenly, the kids from the PTS youth appear with this humongous tent. It was a good way to continue the resistance, although being out in the plaza was very tough—it was quite a few months.

Not long after, the spark in the tent seemed to fade. You got the feeling that the struggle was dying out ...

The compañeras didn't want anything to do with the leftist parties anymore. The unemployed worker organizations left. They all went back to their usual ways. The workers fought with the Left because it was all we had. If the Justicialists (Peronists) had come to help us, we would have never gone with the Left. That's the reason I stopped being Peronist at that time. I went to ask what had been my party to help us and we never got a response. The Left supported us, and helped feed us—helped us survive—using the strike funds. Later, with the change in government, people went back to their usual ways, wanting to be legal again, to return to the cooperative idea. By May or June all the paperwork was done. On top of everything, we had gone to Uruguay to do some research and found that one of the factory's main creditors was an associate of Brukman. It had really been a loan to himself. That was helpful in asking the courts to declare Brukman bankrupt.

What's your evaluation of the Cultural Week that was organized at the tent?

It was the best part of those times. Many people came to show their support—Naomi Klein and other authors. It got press around the world and helped boost our strike fund, which was what we needed the most, so that we could keep up the fight. The idea came from the compañeros at Boedo Film, Kino Nuestra Lucha, and Contraimagen.[21] We got a job out of it too—an order of 2,000 handkerchiefs for the English anti-globalization movement, for a G-8 alternative summit in Mexico.

What did you live off during all those months?

The strike fund. Workers would go to the universities. We could take 50, 80, 100 pesos home. Nevertheless, some left because they had to pay rent or had kids in school. It was tough being there without a regular salary.

What repercussions did your decision to run for the Legislature on the PTS ticket have at the tent?

I decided to accept the nomination because I knew I would have platforms where I could speak and make it known that we wanted the factory back and that we wanted a definitive expropriation law. It was a way to get word out about the struggle. I knew the PTS was a tiny party, I knew my limitations and didn't expect to win.

Why such controversy then?

They didn't give Juan Carlos, who was Polo Obrero's candidate, any trouble. But he didn't appear on any leaflets, posters—nothing. And, all of a sudden, I appeared plastered all over the city. My coworkers never liked me standing out. They said that both the party and I were trying to capitalize on the struggle, but that never affected me.

Some of the workers criticized you, saying that the party had hijacked a fight that belonged to all the workers.

I don't know, it could be. Besides, times had changed by then, the government had changed. People began to see things differently. Many discussions began to break out in the tent—they questioned the lawyers because they hadn't expected or prepared us for the expulsion. And then the cooperative was formed.

What was the turning point?

The same lawyers suggested that perhaps in some legal form we could reenter the factory. Two coworkers went to talk with Eduardo Murúa, but didn't come back very convinced. I talked with the CEPRODH to see if they would go speak with Luis Caro, to see what solution he had. A lot of time had passed and we needed a solution. I made an appointment with him one morning, he spoke with my coworkers, and we decided to let him be our advisor. The only thing we never agreed with him on was point number eight of the Expropriations Law that says that if the strikebreakers want to come back and work, we have to accept them.

But none of them came.

The strikebreakers knew that they couldn't come back, even if the law authorizes them to do so. Every time I spoke to the media I told them that they couldn't come back. There was one time that they came to the factory escorted by a police car, and they got theirs on their way out. We threw stuff at them....

When your coworkers decided to call the Reclaimed Factories Move-

ment, did you at any point think that Brukman was no longer the place for you?

No, no. I kept thinking that this was my place, and I had to fight it out. I fight for what I consider I need to fight for. I fight to convince my coworkers of what I believe. How they vote is another matter. I'm not about to leave because they don't think like I do— I've fought too much for that. My children offered to buy me a sewing machine so I could stay home and work. Another son, who has a bakery, offered to rent me a place to set up a bakery. But no, for me, being here is my life. Being at Brukman is what I bet it all on, what I fought for.

How did you feel the day that you were given the factory's title?

Incredible joy, and also some bitterness. Because many people who should have been there were not—people who struggled and put their bodies on the line. Suddenly the workers weren't the ones speaking. The lawyer spoke, and then a congressman who announced a new law, trying to take political credit for our fight.

And now, how does the internal organization of the cooperative work?

Like always. Now we have a president and a trustee, but we continue to decide everything by assembly—everybody earns the same salary. We're earning between 100 and 150 pesos a week. We have the old customers who always stuck by us, and look for new ones.

Have you ever thought that Brukman is the most famous reclaimed factory in the world and, at the same time, the one whose legal fight lasted the longest?

No, I never thought about that. I always said that we would come back, that we would fight. When the government offered us the option of establishing a small business, we voted no. Nevertheless, a group went to go find out about the offer anyway, to learn what it was about. There was a group of about twenty that wanted to accept the offer. All over again we had to fight, debate, but, for me, it was always about this place. We managed to stop the idea. I believed that the fight was for *this*, not for some place just anywhere. They had beaten us up over this factory and we weren't about to go quietly to a shed in Villa Tachito (poor neighborhood of Greater Buenos Aires). One has to have some pride in what one is fighting for—and be convinced of it. I was always convinced that we would return to this factory.

Why did you and a group of workers call yourselves Brukman dissidents?

The cooperative is in the Movement of Reclaimed Factories. The thing is that some of us don't agree with this. We don't like that only the presidents of the cooperatives can speak in the Movement. Also, there are a lot of important things going on outside the factory and around us that we now ignore. During our struggle people showed so much solidarity with us—and we also stood in solidarity with them. But now we don't even go to the marches. I don't know, maybe joining the MNER has made us more selfish.

Chapter Three

Crometal
Twenty-First Century Metalworkers

After a year-and-a-half-long conflict, a metalworking company that produces industrial shelving and Acrow scaffolds was taken over by the workers of the Crometal Cooperative. Here at the factory, one hears the forgotten clamor of an operating metal factory, and if you listen to the story of these workers, whom the media consistently harassed, who occupied this factory four times and were expelled from it three, who lived on a bus, who will tell you that they know what humiliation is, and whom the bosses tried to buy off with three kilos of meat.

Daniel Martins, 50, with a thick old-fashioned mustache, president of the Crometal Cooperative, recognizes that after so many double-crosses, uncertainties, and surprises, the co-op members have learned how to sleep cautiously—with one eye open.

Martins is an overalls-wearing president. "Here we're all technicians, engineers, workers, whatever." The interview is conducted in an executive meeting room, cold because it's hardly used. "This began in late 2001, together with the *corralito*[1] and de la Rúa's downfall. By then we hadn't been paid in two or three months already. We didn't have a dime. It's something that really gets to you," says Daniel.

Why did this company go under?

It's a mystery when you discover that this factory of industrial shelving had 1,700 customers, including Techint, Arcor, Johnson & Johnson, Sancor, Carrefour, Coto, the Argentine Navy, Andreani, Oca, and Roggio. One interpretation of the company's downfall goes, "Eduardo Nascimento, the owner, has three companies. One is Enas, that rents and sells scaffolds, and a third rents and sells construction materials. It was evident that Acrometálica would purchase raw materials, pay taxes, wages, and bills, but sold nothing. Enas was the one that would sell. [Acrometálica's bankruptcy] was a lockout, a hollowing out of the company. This man's other companies still run, and they sunk this one," says Martins.

What was the deal? "To empty Acrometálica out. He even took a mortgage loan. He got $260,000. He had the company take out the loan, but none of the money ever got here." Jorge Rodríguez, the cooperative's secretary, suggests another element. "It's clear he wanted to shut down production, and at the other companies he would hire people under the table, under very unusual conditions."

The struggle began in late 2001, but in January of 2002 it seemed that it would all be resolved. The company offered the workers 100 pesos a week to pay off what it owed them. The promise lasted two weeks.

Three Kilograms of Meat

The plant's electricity, gas and telephone were shut off because the bills hadn't been paid. The $260,000 loan was still safeguarded from being spent on such necessities.

In the face of this situation, on February 6, 2002, the workers decided to occupy the plant to demand their wages, or at least severance pay, if the company was not planning to continue operating.

In response, two days later, they received telegrams telling them they were fired. Saying it was justified by charging the workers with trespassing, it tacked on a criminal lawsuit against them as well.

And so began a strange dance of conversations, negotiations, and hearings at the Labor Ministry. In March a man named Ricardo Rabin showed up to take charge of the company. "He came with a proposal that we discussed in this very room, right where we're sitting," says Martins. "He represented a Brazilian company, Formet, that was associated with Nascimiento—or so he said—claiming that he came to get the company back on track. He got us thinking that there could be a solution, but he said that he had to study the situation to be able to convince the Brazilians to take over."

Rabin announced that Formet was short the money to pay salaries, and proposed paying them twenty pesos a week and three kilograms (6.6 pounds) of meat.

"We accepted this," Martins confesses, embarrassed, "because we had gone several months without pay, and thought it was a way to help the company and keep our jobs."

Rabin never paid them. The workers soon uncovered the ruse. The "proposals" were a way of wearing down the struggle, and soon the workers discovered a fact that convinced them the company was determined to sabotage the business. "They wanted to rent out the factory grounds as a supermarket warehouse, because of its strategic location between Buenos Aires and La Plata (capital of the province of Buenos Aires). That's how they thought they could get the workers and everything else off their hands."

The workers and "everything else" were still dead set on stopping plans to dismantle the factory. Jorge Rodríguez tells how at that point, the Metallurgical Workers' Union of Quilmes (the county where the factory is located) itself proposed that the workers form a cooperative. They then contacted Horacio Campos, the president of IMPA (the cooperative that retook the factory of the same name), Eduardo Murúa (of the National Movement of Reclaimed Enterprises), and, in April of 2002, created the Crometal Worker Cooperative. The workers won a unanimous vote from the City Council of Berazategui (the Quilmes city where the factory is located) that declared the factory public domain and subject to expropriation, and also received support from the Buenos Aires provincial legislature, which cast its vote for expropriation.

Scared of Thieves

The factory was still occupied and paralyzed. A small group would always stay at night to take care of the facilities, so nothing would get stolen, says Rodríguez.

Were they afraid of thieves?

"No, we were afraid of the boss. Our fear was that they might take something valuable. The compressor, for example, that makes most of the machines work, is worth $50,000. Without the machines we wouldn't ever be able to get the factory back into production."

Two months later they got kicked out.

On June 19, 2002, this was the balance of power:

Outside the fence stood 115 police officers, armed in preparation for the eventuality of a clash, and willing to crush any resistance.

Inside, five workers. Shortly thereafter, those inside left, and those outside went in.

"No, there was no resistance—115 against five, there was nothing to be done," Rodríguez says.

So that's where they stayed—outside. Someone lent them an old orange and white school bus. That was their refuge. Martins says, "We transferred our entire lives to the bus. We cooked, slept, held meetings there—it was like a mobile home."

With their lives relocated, they looked on through the fence as the bosses reoccupied the factory. They stayed in the bus. Since they were still afraid of the bosses taking materials or machinery, they learned the art of sleeping with one eye open.

The bus was the symbol of an unresolved conflict. Rabin proposed negotiation and offered a check for almost 9,000 pesos to reduce their debt. "We accepted it because that way our umbilical cord to the factory wasn't cut," Martins admits. By signing the check, they were ratifying their dependant relationship.

This shows that the cooperative idea could be an expression of their dreams, but the workers were closer to desperation, and open to a conventional solution. One detail: They never cashed the Planes Trabajar so as not to acknowledge their firings. The income of each of these men was equal to zero.

Daniel Martins, with a smile behind his big Nietzschean mustache, highlights something else, "When you get home and realize that your wife can't prepare dinner because she doesn't have anything to make it with…that, at least in my case, as a man, husband, father, makes me feel belittled."

Martins looks at us and asks, "You know what I mean?"

Who Defends the Companies?

The check Rabin gave them bounced. There's a sign in the factory that the old bosses had put up to warn the operators: "Every delay is a waste of time." But during the struggle, the company knew that they bought themselves time and wore the struggle down with every delay. Rabin, a man with a poker face, came again with another proposal that these men—between their natural willingness to be polite and their individual desperation—had the patience to listen to. They remember Rabin as a talkative and picturesque individual, capable of convincing them of things that, in retrospect, turned out to be extremely damaging to them.

The workers accepted the fact that the talks [with Rabin] continued to be literally worthless, so they stayed on the bus, brainstorming other solutions. Since they still had not been paid a cent, they would go out to Route 2 and ask motorists for solidarity donations.

Martins says it more crudely. "We lived off charity. We asked the motorists to take pity on our situation. They would give us some change." They also received some help from IMPA and the UOM-Quilmes (the Metallurgical Workers' Union), led by House Representative Francisco "Barba" Gutiérrez. On the state level, the Polo Social Party[2], with support from Peronist groups, was supporting the idea of expropriating the plant, but nothing was moving along very quickly.

That's how the second occupation of the factory was launched on October 28, 2002. That day the bus was surrounded by representatives from the neighborhood assemblies of Parque Avellaneda and Pompeya, among others, joined by IMPA workers, workers from other factories in Berazategui, people from the UOM, and neighbors.

They simply, together, walked back into the factory. "Barba" Gutiérrez was in charge of the negotiation—in the presence of the police—with Rabin. The workers would keep four representatives inside the plant, and the company would keep its ownership.

One group set itself up in the factory and another stayed on the bus. They continued going out to the highway to explain their situation to the motorists. They estimate that six out of ten drivers put something in their cardboard donation boxes. The other four continued on their way, most of the time, without insulting them.

"Between the neighborhood assemblies, the workers from other factories, and the attitudes of many members of the community, we always felt there were people standing behind us," Martins acknowledges. "Without those people we wouldn't have been able to continue the fight, and each of us would have gone home. That's the truth. But we workers stayed at the plant watching over the company's assets."

The phrase Martins uses seems paradoxical, but this was one of those cases in which the company's assets were too important to leave in the bosses' hands.

In November the House of Representatives passed the workers' Expropriations Law. The bill was in the Senate awaiting consideration when the government decreed that all expropriations had to be compensated—when the time came—by the cooperatives. The bill's wording had to be changed, but summer was approaching.

Piqueteros on Route 2

The demand *"Que se vayan todos"* (they all must go) was strictly obeyed—the legislators all went on vacation.

The workers continued to depend on charity from Route 2. Rodríguez remembers, "Rabin sent some journalists from *La Nación*. On January 2, they published an article saying that we were charging motorists a toll. We weren't even blocking the road—we left one lane open. We only obstructed traffic to ask for donations and then let people go on their way. But the *La Nación*

Deciding What's News

On June 18, 2003, lavaca.org presented a report on freedom of expression in Argentina to Eduardo Bertoni, representative of the Inter-American Human Rights Commission (CIDH). One of its key points was its denunciation of the fact that the occupied factories only made news when their workers were expelled from their workplaces: "That limits the possibility of reporting on their new conditions of production or of fostering a public debate about what policies and resources would improve their functioning."

One example was the reopening of the metalworking factory Crometal. "Until this reopening, the workers only appeared in the media as 'those unemployed people who charged tolls to allow passage on Route 2' (according to *La Nación*). By contrast, not a single mainstream media outlet reported the factory's reopening at the end of the conflict."

article made us look really bad."

The next day the area was filled with police cars and television vans that really did block traffic. "There were media that supported us, like *El Sol*, of Quilmes, or *Diario Popular*. But most were against us. They would say we were piqueteros—all kinds of things. After the *La Nación* thing, the television channels came and wanted to show how we blocked the road. It hurt quite a bit, because they were just kicking us when we were already down. They wanted us to be actors in a play that they directed themselves. Now whenever they threw us out of the plant, not a single journalist was there. And it makes you think, 'what country are we living in?' "

Martins doesn't let it get to him. "It's best not to even remember the most terrible things."

The *La Nación* article made the local police out to be pretty much the workers' accomplices. Consequently, the so-called forces of law and order had to overact in the opposite direction. So they surrounded the factory to prevent the workers from going near Route 2. Before, the police lines were for keeping the workers from entering the plant. Now, they kept them from leaving. On March 3rd, the workers decided to chain themselves to the door, to keep the bosses from taking any more stock or machinery, something that they had previously done while accompanied by the Buenos Aires Police Department. Rabin argued that he had a warrant to remove materials.

By the time Representative Gutiérrez managed to verify that there was no such warrant, the workers and UOM members chained to the door had already been invited to experience the hospitality of Buenos Aires's jails. They were locked up for one day.

The situation went back to the previous unstable equilibrium—some of the cooperative's workers continued guarding the factory from a possible stripping of its assets. Two weeks later everything changed.

Shotguns and Doctrine

There were nine of them. One got out of a red Fiat Duna with a long shotgun. Another burly man stepped out of a Citróen van with an ax in each hand. The other seven also brandished their weapons. The third car was a white Fiat 128, Daniel Martins recalls.

Rabin led the group.

The one with the shotgun didn't mince words—up on his soapbox—he yelled, "Get out of here or I'll shoot your balls off."

It was sundown, the time when they maintained the smallest workers' patrol. The armed gang confronted Jorge Rodriguez's tired stare and Daniel Martins' increasingly graying mustache.

Both workers decided that the most prudent response was to return to the old orange and white bus on the other side of the fence. "From there we could see how those thugs walked around inside the factory with Rabin."

That was the second expulsion.

Two days later, the third occupation took place. The neighbors of Berazategui, several Buenos Aires neighborhood assemblies, workers from other reclaimed factories—between 100 and 200 people—gathered once again on the other side of the fence.

The thugs—including the burly man with the two axes— didn't brandish their weapons this time. Martins doesn't think this was for formal or legal reasons. "It would have been too risky to use their weapons against so many people. They wouldn't have even had time to reload."

The gang was forced out and the workers situated themselves inside the factory once again. The company, beyond these legal, violent, and police-backed cartwheels, never tried to resolve the conflict through the farfetched means of recognizing the workers' rights.

Finally, on April 8, 2003, the temporary Expropriations Law was signed. The Crometal workers, using old materials, started working to get the machines running and plan the grand opening of their new enterprise. They didn't even have time to celebrate— and they continued to sleep with one eye open.

The third expulsion occurred on May 14, 2003. Provincial Judge Marcelo Goldberg ordered the disruption and eviction of the workers from the factory. "We were working when we saw the police arrive with the eviction warrant. We didn't understand anything anymore," tells Rodríguez.

"We asked what was going on, but the police said to ask at the courthouse. But since it was after 3 p.m., there was nobody at the courthouse."

It makes sense—throwing workers out on the street should not get in the way of the much-deserved rest for members of the judiciary.

The criminal trespassing charges had been collected. Judge Goldberg, who had ordered the first expulsion, together with a prosecutor by the name of Madina, did not give up, despite the existence of a law passed by the Legislature and signed by the Executive branch.

Escorted by Buenos Aires's finest, the unshakable Ricardo

Rabin ostentatiously took charge of the factory once again while the workers looked on from the outside.

This time the workers filed a lawsuit against the judge himself, for obstruction of justice, which could turn into a political trial.

The next day Judge Goldberg met with Representative Gutiérrez and the cooperative's lawyers with a remorseful air. "He said he hadn't seen the Official Bulletin nor the Expropriations Law, despite the fact that they were included in the lawsuit."

It is true that looking at official bulletins and expropriation laws can be cumbersome, but that is what a judge's job is supposed to entail. This judge had over a month to do so. But, faced with a new filing by Rabin and his buddies requesting the eviction, he efficiently applied the law in that direction. As one can see, justice is not always slow.

Martins speculates, "He must have seen the case called 'Acrometálica versus the workers' and said 'throw them out and then we'll see,' I suppose. You can see the man isn't very competent at his job."

But this time Judge Goldberg had provoked a power struggle, ignored a law, and stuck his neck out, risking a political trial.

So he apologized to the workers and declared himself a defender of human rights and public resources.

A Moral Issue

The judge reversed the eviction, approved the Expropriations Law and, for a fourth time, the workers took over the company. This time, not only legitimately, but also with formal legality on their side. Rabin and his gang retreated out of the same front door.

The problem, according to Martins, is that in these cases you get into a legal spiderweb that shows that—on top of determination, willpower, and an immeasurable dose of courage—you have to follow the dispute with a meticulous knowledge of the law in order to reach your objective.

They started the plant back up again. It occupies 20,000 meters (about 65,600 feet) on a 70,000-square-meter (about 750,000 square feet) property. There are tunnels for rinsing the metals, a cabin where robots apply paint, a 40-meter oven that reaches 180°C (356°F). The workers show off the $50,000 compressor, the $10,000 torches, the heavy shelving that supermarket warehouses use, light shelving, scaffolds, structures, and supports used for construction.

Over time they recovered some of the old customers. Without help, without marketing, without subsidies, pure sweat, Martins says. Many businesses work with the cooperatives because they find in them a seriousness and efficiency that doesn't exist among the entrepreneurs bent on asset stripping.

For Martins, the recovery was not just industrial, "Many of us were psychologically worn down. Our way of recovering was not to go to a psychologist but to work here."

Another worker tells how they want to begin to settle down. "Our goal at this point is to be able to live off our work, and we're doing it. But it's not just about money. It's become a moral question. We want to continue showing the Berazategui community, the people who know us, the shopkeepers, the merchants, everyone who gave us a hand, that what they did was really important. Without them we would have fallen apart—and without the assemblies and the factories and the union. We want to tell them this: you weren't wrong about us."

He says it out loud, amidst the din of the machines making scaffolds, and looking out of the corner of his eye, at the old school bus. It's about to be returned to its owner because they will no longer cross the fence to see things from the other side.

Chapter Four

Chilavert
The Things You Have to Do to Work

A print shop managed to overcome years of under production and deterioration, and one day, was about to—literally—go up in flames. How its workers managed to evade the police in order to work.

There is a 20 to 25cm (8–10 inch) peephole in the print shop's wall that has been covered by bricks.

Like every decent peephole, it once served a secret, conspiratorial, and perhaps subversive purpose. In this case, it allowed the print shop's eight workers to work. The undercover activity was performed behind the backs of eight police officers and one security guard, all of whom guarded the building.

Not long ago, these same workers had faced a police siege. But from the building's tall windows, armed with gasoline (among other things), they swore they would burn the whole place down, from the barricade placed at the entrance of the building to the machines and everything else. To this day, when Cándido González tells the story, it brings him to tears.

The workers' assessment was the following: "Blood will be shed, but it will be on both sides."

This story does not come from a politically correct movie about strikes, heroic deeds, and resistance. It happened in the city of Buenos Aires, at what is perhaps one of the best print shops in the country today. It's located in the neighborhood of Pompeya, at 1136 Chilavert Street. The original group was formed by Plácido Peñarrieta, Aníbal Figueroa, Ernesto González, Fermín González, Jorge Luján, Manuel Basualdo, Daniel Suárez, and Cándido González. Cándido and Fermín are brothers.

Cándido is the secretary and a kind of natural spokesperson for the Worker Cooperative. The company's original name was Gaglianone, a popular and high-quality printer that after seventy-six years in existence ended up in the hands of its second generation owner, Horacio Gaglianone. The company entered a crisis, like so many others in Argentina, thanks to the government's behavior and its economic policies in recent decades. But, according to González, there was a revelation on top of all this—Horacio Gaglianone's conscience had died.

At one opportunity, Mr. Gaglianone announced his new priorities to the workers: "I'm going to save myself first, myself second, and myself third." Facing such an action plan, the workers prepared for difficult times.

González refers to Gaglianone's "dead conscience," alluding to what happened when Gaglianone's wife, Tola, died. "She was the one who brought morality to the print shop. Tola died and the guy was left without a conscience. She would go to hospitals to help sick people, she was a generous person, there was something in her."

The owner's attitude turned hostile. "I admit that you want to save yourself, but what about the people who stood beside you your whole life? I'm not saying you should pay them everything, but pay them half or a quarter."

What he says exemplifies the degree of violence that has been perpetrated on these normally even-tempered workers. Cándido, fifty-nine years old, started working at Gaglianone thirty-five years ago. "I never thought it would close." His personal story coincides with those of many more Argentine workers in the last few decades. While very young—in the 1960s—in addition to working, he was active in the unions. He was in the Argentine CGTA[1] and in the Graphic Union.

"Raymundo Ongaro[2] was a fighter," he says, but recognizes that with the leader's exile in the 1970s, union habits changed. "There was an internal struggle—thugs wanted to take over the union. I didn't like any of that and continued as a delegate here at Gaglianone to discuss the working conditions, overtime, breaks, those kinds of things." Then he clarifies his statement, "Ongaro was a fighter, but now he's done us wrong."

That is how Cándido spent the last few decades during the return to democracy. He takes a critical look at himself:

"You concentrate on your own things, on improving your lot, and that's how you begin to distance yourself. It's like you close up and lose touch with reality. That is what happened to us—we lost touch with reality and things passed us by. Now you realize. 'What an idiot. How did I not see the way things were?'"

Cándido began to see things differently after December 19th and 20th, 2001. He began participating in the Pompeya Neighborhood Assembly. "I saw the unemployment problem, the hunger, and I didn't want to stand on the sidelines. I liked that business of working in the neighborhoods, not just protesting."

And then, the unexpected occurred. "I helped gather food for people in need, but in the end, we had to use the food ourselves, so we could eat."

He has adopted the lesson as his motto: "To defend your job, you must defend someone else's job. And to defend your food, you must defend someone else's food."

The Corrupt Orchestra

The story had been unfolding in stages. First, the company went to a creditors' meeting. Cándido explains, "The guy was paying the creditors under the table so he could walk away with the machines. It wasn't a run-of-the-mill bankruptcy, but rather, a stripping of the plant. They fixed the meeting and arranged everything with the judge. That's where corruption begins. And it continues with the judge's secretary and with the corrupt trustee, and on and on, to corrupt accountants and lawyers."

The scheme culminates with a company reduced to an empty plant, like a broken shell. "And the poor owner appears to be a man who has nothing in his name. Nothing can be seized from him, and he can't go to prison. With the judge, they prearrange to drop the machines from the inventory and the company is left empty. These are illegal associations—it's asset stripping."

The event that unleashed the end of it all was when Gaglianone lost the 25-year-old contract to print the programs for the Teatro Colón. "That brought in lots of money with the publicity. I think it was lost because there were a lot of politics involved. You have to pay the guy who arranged the contract with the government, you know what I mean?" (Understood. Chilavert, now a cooperative, has ditched those practices. Now, "We work with the state, but it's just another customer who pays 50 percent before and 50 percent after the job is done.")

Once the Colón contract fell through, Mr. Gaglianone announced that everything would continue as planned, including a change of machinery. "We were here for many weeks without getting paid and with an accumulating debt, but we kept working. Meanwhile, he maneuvered to free up the mortgaged machinery. Since he couldn't take the building, he took the machines."

The Ugly Truth

Cándido explains that this is how the plant's stripping was being planned. From 2000 to 2002 there was hardly any work, the bills were piling up, and Gaglianone announced that he would sell the machines to buy new ones. "We thought it was a normal thing; we were determined to stay with the company. But we suspected something was up when they cut off the electricity."

The workers went to the owner and demanded an explanation of what was going on. It was April 3, 2002. "The guy tells us: 'Boys, you see the mess this country is in. This is going to hell and

I can't buy new machines.' We told him not to buy them, but that he couldn't take the ones that were up for auction. And he answers: 'Who said they were up for auction? I sold them two months ago.' "

Cándido and his coworkers understood: "This guy wants to screw us."

The next day a local mechanic came to dismantle the machines. The workers surrounded them. Gaglianone then appeared with a workshop supervisor and a manager:

"Hey, Cándido, what's this about you not letting me take the machines, how long have we known each other?"

"Excuse me sir, the truth is I don't know you."

"What do you mean you won't let us take them?"

"They're not leaving this place," Cándido explained, with his seven coworkers behind him.

"Okay, let us disconnect them," Gaglianone requested.

"No. If you want to disconnect them, pay us what you owe us."

"How much is it?" the owner asked.

"In my case, 33,000 pesos," explained Cándido. The mechanic's eyes got as wide as saucers, he said goodbye, and he left.

"I warn you that judges can be bought," Gaglianone said, "they'll come with four assault vehicles and throw you out with a swift kick in the ass."

"Okay, when the judge and the assault vehicles come, we'll help them dismantle the machines."

That day, April 4th, they spent the night in the plant, next to the machines. "That's when we jumped the fence. The fence of indecision—we said, 'We're going to fight.' "

When the weekend came and Gaglianone saw that the workers were prepared to spend it in the plant, he understood that it was too late to turn back. "We found a mattress and some furniture upstairs and started to organize ourselves. Gaglianone kept coming. He would lock himself in his office and take the company books home with him. He would still give us one or two peso vouchers and one time he paid us with a US$50 bill that, on top of everything, was counterfeit. When they cut off the telephone, we wired ourselves into the main phone line so we could be in contact with the Pompeya Assembly and with some other assemblies that we had contacted, in case we needed help. One day he heard the phone ring, and he approached us and asked, 'Boys, would you let me make a short call?' After that, we didn't let him take anything else. His position was weakening and we wanted control over everything."

Cándido can't help but define the situation in terms of a war. "One day the corrupt accountant came to take some account books and we shut the door in his face. You lose respect for those people. It's a war, they want to save themselves, and so do we. Everyone defended what was theirs."

What Do You Need to Liquidate a Business?

In those days the workers discovered a magic act:

"The machines were not listed in the inventory compiled at the creditors' meeting. We filed the report against an attempted liquidation, and the trustee said, 'It can't be, I went to the print shop and the machines weren't there.' That proves that there has to be a corrupt judge, a corrupt trustee, and everyone else too, in order to carry out the bankruptcy."

On May 10, 2002, bankruptcy was declared.

"That meant that they could kick us out at any given moment."

At about the same time, they had contacted the National Movement of Reclaimed Companies (MNER) and its president, Eduardo Murúa. The IMPA company and neighborhood assemblies such as Palermo Viejo, Congreso, Parque Avellaneda, and Parque Patricios, among others, were also on the alert.

They began to arrive at the idea of constituting themselves as a cooperative. "Chilavert is the name of the street that we're on, but it is named after the colonel who fought at the Vuelta de Obligado.[3] We liked it for both reasons." Everyone also admits that the fame of the Paraguayan goalie[4] helped to increase our name recognition.

In order to survive, they sold aluminum plates to IMPA. But, unexpectedly, they also received a job to print and bind the cover for the book ¿Qué son las asambleas populares? (What Are Popular Assemblies?), published by Peña Lillo. "But the next day the trustee shows up with three police cars. We called the people from the Pompeya Assembly. We were inside with the trustee while the folks from the assembly saw a locksmith changing the lock on the front door. They stopped him. We'll say they convinced him—he removed the new lock, put the old one back on, and hightailed it out of there. As the IMPA people started showing up, the police were increasingly becoming a minority."

The trustee argued against the workers' intention to take over the company. He said that they didn't even have electricity. However, they had already acquired a small generator with some of the money from the aluminum they sold. "We shut him up with that, and they left, promising to return three days later."

Working Is for Criminals

They continued full throttle with the printing of the book, and two days later, on May 24, 2002, the trustee returned, better escorted than ever before: eight police cars, eight assault vehicles, two ambulances, and a fire truck. "As if we were criminals or terrorists," Cándido describes. The workers sounded their alarms and summoned families, IMPA workers, assembly members (from the Pompeya, Traful, Parque Patricios, Palermo Viejo, and Parque Avellaneda Assemblies), seniors from the neighborhood's retirement center, community members—some 300 people. All came to stand by the eight workers.

They formed a barricade using tires and paper. "We met the force of their assault vehicles with the force of our barricade," Cándido says, beginning to get emotional as he remembers the event.

The workers' wives positioned themselves on the second floor and tossed little pieces of paper from the windows to feed the burning barricade below. "We warned the police that we would burn everything down," Cándido says.

The catch was that they were really prepared to do it. "There were two of us who knew what we had to do. We were going to light the machines on fire. The IMPA people told us, 'We're going to defend you—how far are you willing to go?' "

Cándido's eyes begin to water now as he remembers. We are in the print shop, it's 7 p.m. and it is getting dark, as if trying to hide his tears. He lifts his head and says, "You fight for yourself, but when others fight for you…"

Around 6 or 7 p.m., the judge ordered the workers to evacuate the print shop.

Side Note

The man who received the order was a commissioner who became infamous a few months later. Juan Carlos Pereyra was the commissioner of Police Station #34, where nine police officers were charged with throwing teenagers into the Riachuelo[5] (a contaminated river on the edge of the federal capital), killing one of them, Ezequiel Demonty.

Cándido says, "I knew this Pereyra guy because he had come to the Pompeya Assembly representing Mauricio Macri, to invite the neighbors for a hot chocolate. In those times he was already campaigning for Macri, even though he was an active commissioner."

All interpretations about the relationship between "Commissioner Pereyra," "Macri," "chocolate," and "teenagers thrown into the Riachuelo," are left to the reader.

"Don't Start the Fire"

Commissioner Pereyra received the order to evict as he watched the barricade and heard supporters from the community. "The people were insulting the police," Cándido describes. He begged the workers, "Don't start the fire." He told the judge, "Look, there are a lot of people."

On the second floor, the workers had placed gasoline drums near the windows, among other things, planning to defend themselves.

"We told ourselves: blood will be shed, but on both sides." Finally, it seems that the commissioner managed to convince the judge. The television cameras also seem to have been influential. At 10 p.m., the Chilavert siege was lifted by the so-called forces of law and order, leaving eight agents as guards. (The police obsession with the number eight eludes Cándido and his seven coworkers.)

The Peephole

For two months the group of eight police officers remained at the plant door to impede suspicious activities, primarily, working. It was a way of breaking down the stubbornness of those who had jumped the fence.

Cándido describes what they did next. "The book about the assemblies was still in process. We decided to print the covers. Gaglianone had left behind a private security guard whom we chatted up so that he wouldn't see anything. We justified the fact that the machines were running by saying that they had to be turned on so they wouldn't be ruined. We did the job, but we couldn't get the books out. We thought of taking them up through the roof, but a neighbor offered to break a hole through the wall and take them out through his house. We made the hole and then a neighbor took us to deliver them in his car, because we didn't even have money for the bus. One day, as we were passing the books through the hole, someone said, 'Look at the things you have to do to work.' "

The hole is about two meters above ground, where there was once an air conditioner. The workers took advantage of that space to break the wall again and pass the books through it. On the other side, the neighbor, Don Julio Berlusconi, received them. He makes a funny face when he says that his last name is Berlusconi. "What can you do about it? For a guy like Berlusconi to govern Italy shows that the world has gone crazy."

Don Julio has a small metal workshop in his house. By opening that hole in the wall, he was committing a crime. "But I'm a
worker and that is what matters. If I have to help a comrade, then
I help him, and that's it," he points out.

To camouflage the hole in Chilavert, the workers hung a
framed de la Cárcova still life.

The painting is now hung as a keepsake below the peephole,
which has now been filled in with bricks. It will stay that way forever, exposed, in order to not be forgotten: *naturaleza viva*.[6]

Marketing and Fun

Slowly, they began to get the company back on its feet and
they also began taking home a decent wage (first 200 pesos a
month, building up to the current 800). They achieved the unexpected. "We went to all the protests to show our solidarity and
Chilavert gained the reputation of being a print shop belonging to
the struggle. Our propaganda was word of mouth, it was our marketing," says Cándido.

They don't count on the support of the Graphic Union led by
Raymundo Ongaro. González points out, "He was a fighter, but
what he is now…"

Cándido sticks his hand in his pocket and pulls out two bills.
One is bluish, like the two-peso bill, with an image of a man wearing a turban and with characters similar to those in the Russian al-
phabet. The other is green like a dollar, with the supposed value of
"one million dollars," written in letters and numbers.

I ask him what that bill is all about. "Ongaro gave them to us
as a password to be able to negotiate with the welfare people with
his backing. As if out of pity, he gave us two months' welfare and

said that we were on our own after that." Ongaro is not one of the men who jumped the fence. "No, how's he going to jump anyways? He's monkeying around way over there and he'll never get anywhere. I don't know what happened to him; he used to be different. I kept the fake bills as souvenirs."

The workers at Chilavert make less money than in the old days. "But we have fun, because we do our own things. It's a different environment, a different relationship. None of us would consider working under a boss again."

Cándido thinks that although the reclaimed factories and companies are a small speck within the universe of the Argentine economy, "The difference is that we are a prestigious little speck. Not all who have a lot of power have prestige."

Cándido describes the new situation—they achieved the final expropriation of the plant on November 25, 2004—talks about the future, and sums up the experience with a few words that are best not forgotten:

"You know what was the most important thing for us? *Feeling that we can do it.*"

Chapter Five

Sime
Quarry of Resistance

Sime Quarry, in Victoria, Entre Ríos Province, was expropriated and reclaimed by its workers. At times, they suffered extreme humiliation and workplace abuse, but when they took the place into their own hands, they managed to reverse a destiny headed toward unemployment. They came out armed and ready to fight, sustaining themselves on hunting, fishing, and solidarity. Today they have managed to reactivate a plant that had been crippled by asset stripping, evasion, and the kinds of traps the workers believed only happened on TV.

The province of Entre Ríos was once at the bottom of the ocean. No one knows what a world at such depths looked like. Even with the benefits of modern science, we are better off using our imagination to try to picture it. Perhaps it was a place more hospitable for its inhabitants—creatures with fewer dilemmas than those of today.

But millions of years ago, a tumult of events took place. The earth came unhinged, the continents rose, fell, and scattered across the planet. Finally, it emerged, a fact that is often lost in a region dominated by its political and economic events.

Fresh water, rivers, and new forms of life and death appeared. Eventually, an enigmatic biped began to take over the region.

Among the emerged territories is one called Argentina, which includes an area known as Entre Ríos, wherein lies a section that goes by the name of Victoria. If you dig four meters down, you find sea snails, oysters, and shells. An ocean formed by tons of souvenirs from a prehistory that can only be imagined. And if you look only at the surface, you find the nightmares and hopes of those about whom we should leave a record to aid future archaeologists.

The Sime Quarry, in Victoria, 92 kilometers (57 miles) from the city of Paraná, the capital of Entre Ríos, functioned for half a century extracting seashells and petrified oysters (pure calcium carbonate) used for cow feed, asphalt, and road repairs. (Route 11, which connects the provinces of Santa Fé, Chaco, and Formosa, has a stretch called "the white road," paved with this material.) But mainly it was used for chicken feed. The calcium carbonate, mixed with a balanced diet, strengthens the birds so that they lay healthy eggs with strong shells.

After decades of normal operation, the quarry's last executives managed to destroy the business, paralyze the plant, and leave its workers on the street and its clients without supplies—a company fatally destined to break eggs.[1]

María del Huerto, 45, relates the story in a sweet accent with Guaraní[2] echoes. At times she becomes angry and indignant at the events, as she recalls, "In December of 2002 they gave us a 35-day unscheduled vacation. We refused because they couldn't tell us and not inform the clients or suppliers. We went to the Labor Ministry and the miners' union and a deferred payment contract was signed." It was December 23rd. The company asked to postpone the meeting. "See how cold-blooded they are? They left us with nothing for Christmas," she says. The meeting was postponed until December 30. "And they did the same thing there."

The mandatory vacations lasted until January 20th. The twenty-eight workers returned to the quarry in the silence of the countryside and found it empty. "A pasture with no lights, running water, or telephone service. Nothing. It was desolate." All that remained were a few old machines.

Weapons in Hand

María had already met with members of the Movement of Reclaimed Companies, "I didn't know that you could occupy a factory or a company. They told me that the slogan is 'occupy, resist, and produce,' and that changed my life." Complying with the first two points of the slogan, María and her coworkers took back the quarry, weapons in hand—"in case we had to resist," she explains. "We took firearms, and some neighbors lent us shotguns. We announced that we didn't want to shoot anyone, but wanted to defend our workplace and keep the bosses from stealing anything else."

What did the word "resistance" mean? It was summer, when the sticky heat could reach 40°C [104°F], mosquitoes were rampant, and the workers had no income. "To eat, the men hunted *apereá* rabbits—they're brown; they look like big mice. They also fished *caruchas* from a nearby lagoon, and Don Joaquín would send us tarpon fish from the market. What had happened to us? We thought of ourselves as middle class, and here we were, begging and hunting to make ends meet."

Hunting, fishing, and solidarity. The Benedictine Abbey, which operates a hostel, prepared food in bulk for the guests and also for the workers, who, in order to make some money, hunted red-and-yellow-crested cardinals in the quarry, selling them for five pesos apiece.

Workplace Abuse

Before continuing with the story, there is one question that comes to mind: How did the situation reach this point? María recalls, "The quarry changed ownership in the late 1990s, and Mr. Roberto Vizioli was left in charge. When he died, his spouse, María Enriqueta Fontán, a clerk from Avellaneda (a county in Greater Buenos Aires), took over. This woman's daughter, Mariquita Sánchez Fontán, was brought in as manager. We later discovered that they were not owners. The stock was under a mason's name. And they also established a ghost company, San Roberto, under the name of one of their domestic servants." The picture was completed with the discovery of the purchase of a machine made under the name of El Chino Quarries. The workers found out from the Federal Administration of Public Incomes (AFIP) that that alleged company—located in the exact same place as the Sime Quarry—belonged to an octogenarian acting as a front. "The place was being stripped clean and full of corruption. It's what we inherited from the Menem era," María reasons. She also experienced a particularly hostile situation at the factory itself.

Cecilia, who worked with María in the administrative offices, felt it first. "The clerk and her daughter Mariquita screamed at us, insulted us. Mariquita wasn't normal, she screamed all the time and paced back and forth like a crazy person. We later found out that they had sent her for therapy. Unfortunately, her idea of therapy was abusing the workers." As a result, Cecilia had to go into treatment. "She developed a kind of persecution complex, a phobia. She would shut herself up in her house, afraid she'd run into the Fontáns on the street."

María describes the problem frankly, "It was workplace abuse. It's the same as when there is a husband that beats his wife. You live that way, in a state of permanent submission and fear." Cecilia, who has three kids, left the job. María was left alone at the quarry. "That's when they came down on me," María said.

What did the mistreatment consist of? "They would scream things like 'son of a thousand bitches, you're good for nothing!' Sometimes point-blank into my ear. You would think they were about to hit you, but you had to just bite your tongue. You know why? To keep your job. I had been working at the plant for twenty-three years."

Things worsened when the bosses transferred María to a different job. "The truckers were quitting en masse. I was given money to pay them—one peso for each ton they transported. They responded to me, 'Ma'am, do you expect us to work for free?' "

"Mariquita called from Buenos Aires and screamed, 'Have you hired any truckers yet, you piece of shit?' "

"'No, Mariquita, no one will take the job at that price.' "

"'You good-for-nothing whore. You're doing this on purpose. You better hope I don't find you when I get there.' "

"When I hung up the phone, I felt something strange, like my heart was going to burst. I called a taxi and they took me to the Victoria Policlinic. The doctor put a pill under my tongue and said, 'María, you can't go on this way; that woman is deranged, she's sick, her brain is mush. Think about your health.' "

María went home and returned to the quarry a couple of days later, thinking that things would have calmed down. "It was worse. The mother and the daughter together told me all kinds of things: 'You good-for-nothing, worthless whore, we need a fleet of trucks for transport, but you won't call them because you're a piece-of-shit idiot who lives with her ass glued to a chair. I hope you die soon.' All of it right in my ear! I lasted until 4 p.m., shaking, and then my husband took me to a neurologist. They transferred me to a psychiatrist, where they gave me sedatives and psychological support."

Despite everything María recounts, she falters only when describing what she refers to as a "photograph." "I saw, from the office window, a coworker, Walter Saldaña. They had put him out in the sun to break rocks and shells with a hammer. The only thing missing were the shackles. I'll never forget that photograph."

Shortly thereafter, the quarry closed and the workers were furloughed, and María told her former coworker Cecilia, "These women are going to leave us on the street, why don't we go see how we can help?"

Hitting Bottom and Bouncing Back

María found out about reclaimed companies because of an award won by Jorge Aguilera, a worker for the Rosario-based company Mil Hojas.

"I found the man through the Telecom 110 (information number) and set up an appointment with him. I met him along with José Abelli and other workers who had reclaimed their factories. I learned what the word 'lockout' meant, which I hadn't heard before."

María learned how to investigate, detect fronts, and convince legislators. "We discovered that the company had been evading taxes. One of our coworkers filed for retirement and found the company had not paid any of the money they had been deducting from his paycheck over the last nine years."

The workers formed the Sime Quarry Worker Cooperative, elected María del Huerto as its president, and, in April of 2003, a judge ordered that the plant be put under the trusteeship of the cooperative. "We had been drawing unemployment subsidies that paid us 160 pesos, but now we were able to truly start working. I'm thankful that none of my coworkers committed suicide, that we didn't lose anyone on the way, because they were already selling their furniture in order to buy meat, you know? It's depressing— it's belittling."

They were also able to stop hunting rabbits and cardinals. A group of students from the medical school visited them, treating them almost like subjects in an experiment. "They told me that every worker that has gone through the recovery of a company has psychologically hit bottom. On the other hand, work has now changed our lives. You see that workers are happier, more dynamic. We proved that being dark-skinned riff-raff from Entre Ríos doesn't mean that we're dumb, because we didn't let ourselves get trampled on. Nor did we let ourselves continue to be treated like beggars."

María's husband, Juan Ángel Schwindt, also works at the Sime Quarry. They have three kids, ages 10, 17, and 19. "Who would've guessed that, at our age, we were going to cry because of the anguish together, and then cry for joy together when we reclaimed the quarry. I didn't know those things happened. Well, I saw them on TV. But now it happened to me."

María recognizes that this was the second time her job has saved her. Before it happened because of a different kind of emptying. "I was diagnosed with uterine cancer, so they performed a hysterectomy. After the operation I went with my husband to the doctor who had the surgery results on the table and a worried look on his face. I said:

Coco, what is it? Am I doing badly?

No, María, worse. I took your uterus out for nothing. It was a mistake; the uterus was clean.

My husband wanted to kill him on the spot. But, since I was there with the stitches and all, it ended there."

María subsequently suffered premature menopause, accompanied by dry skin problems, weakening bones, and—fundamentally—a depression that kept her from leaving the house. "I was a witch without a broom. One day I looked in the mirror and said—that's not me. You know what I did? I went to the hairdresser, did my makeup, put on my heels, and went to work. They didn't want to let me. I told them, 'if you want me to get better, let me work.'"

The Work, Before and After

María and her coworkers wrote to each and every representative and senator, and won expropriation of the quarry in a unanimous vote by both houses of the state parliament. It was August 22, 2004. "Everyone was there. The Benedictines, the customers, the police, and the local journalists, who treated us very fairly." Victoria honored its name.

The workers are today extracting 1,600 tons, compared to the 2,000 tons they produced when the plant closed. "We regained our credibility and customers. The truth is that they all helped us and even lent us hectares of land to continue extracting shells." The workers started taking home 50 pesos a week each, and maintained the unemployment fund. "We're starting over. I sent a letter to President Kirchner because we need a backhoe loader. Right now we are renting one that costs us 60 pesos an hour—7,000 pesos a week—that could be going toward our income." They paid the bills and the quarry has electricity once again. "It's just that it's time we react, get up, and say 'Enough!' We workers can't stay home crying about our misfortunes when they've stripped us of the human right to work." The cooperative is filing lawsuits against all the old owners, since they also have to be paid the severance pay they never received. "We also have to beat the swindlers in Buenos Aires, because when you go to the AFIP, you discover that everything is controlled by fronts, you know?"

The workers now have the plant and the old machines. They executed those words that they didn't know they could make their own—they occupied, they resisted, and they are producing. Research is trying to determine if calcium carbonate also has pharmacological uses, which could give the plant a new product line. The shells are 98 percent calcium carbonate, which could serve as a raw material for medicines to treat osteoporosis, or even malnutrition. Bioengineering students from Oro Verde (an Entre Ríos university town) have proposed that a generic drug laboratory to manufacture this kind of medicine could be established. Where the resources (which would serve to generate many more resources), the political will, the support for this project, and the decency to create more jobs will come from, no one knows. Their future is as uncertain as anyone else's in these uncharted territories, but—as María says—they no longer cry over their misfortunes, but rather, they leave the madness and abuse behind. "Who would have guessed it? With the stroke of a pen they crushed our hopes. But even at this age, I'm learning how to start over."

Chapter Six

Conforti
The Rebellion of the Machines

*One of the country's biggest printing companies came back to life
thanks to the efforts of a group of workers who, after facing the abyss
of unemployment, managed to expropriate the plant and put it back
in motion. This is the story of how they overcame a scheming businessman and a court system that looked the other way. Today, in addition to the print shop, there is a graphic arts school to reincorporate
adolescents into the educational system, a cultural center, and a
neighborhood library.*

In mid-2003, the walls of the green building that occupies
half a block on Patricios Avenue 1900, in Barracas, Buenos Aires,
described the situation at the Conforti Graphic Shop in just a
few words. White capital letters informed:

*CONFORTI WORKERS WANT TO KEEP OUR JOBS.
THEY OWE US OVER A YEAR IN WAGES. NO TO LIQUI-
DATION!!*

*JUSTICE FOR THE WORKERS!! WE WANT A SOLUTION
NOW!!*
   MORE THAN THREE MONTHS OF STRUGGLE.
   RAÚL GONZALO, CRIMINAL, PAY UP!
   NO TO PLANNED BANKRUPTCIES.
   NO EVICTION.
   There was also a proposal that was a model of precision and
harmony, in light of the effect that these situations provoke:
   *GONZALO, YOU SON-OF-A-BITCH THIEF, PAY UP
WHAT YOU OWE.*
   And at the end, the two most profound words (they become
four when translated into English) were painted in white over
green:
   WE WANT TO WORK.[1]
   Barracas is one of Buenos Aires's oldest neighborhoods, with
blocks elevated from street level to avoid succumbing to floods.
Conforti is half a block from the Riachuelo. Its lowered shutters
look like the closed eyes of a company in a coma, a victim of another kind of flooding and of one of those business corruption
cases that are emblematic of the so-called "national leadership"
(that is, if those two words still make any sense together).

Killing Time

   The meeting with the Patricios Graphic Cooperative workers
is in a quiet, dark, and idle workshop, which is the greatest sadness
for any graphic artist or journalist. The movie *Terminator 3* revives
a classic science fiction theme—the rebellion of machines as an
omen of human catastrophe. In Argentina, the catastrophe has al-

ready occurred and the rebellion of the machines is, in any case, what will allow factories and workshops like Conforti to function once again. Here we follow a different script, where machines and humans are allies.

In the workshop the machines are quiet, with their eyes shut. The workers are playing cards. Essentially, the game is always the same—it's about killing time, to keep time from killing them. But there is something that overcomes this silence—the workers estimate that in twenty days this situation can decisively transform into a much louder environment. Along with the machines, they will regain their ability to work.

The story began to fall apart between 1998 and 1999 when the president of Conforti, Raúl Gonzalo, began paying his workers the bare minimum. He is a pudgy, driven, and slick man who always had a beard and drove a 4x4. "He's the kind of guy who convinces you that everything that is yours is his, and you believe him," say the workers.

There was no shortage of work.

Gustavo Ojeda, a union delegate who is now a member of the Patricios Graphic Cooperative that the workers have formed, remembers that among the print shop's clients were *El Cronista Comercial* newspaper, *Cablevisión, Telecentro,* and *Segundamano* magazines, and an in-flight magazine called *Vía Aérea,* to name a few. It's clear that there wasn't a work shortage—there was a *salary* shortage. Some eighty workers put up with pay cuts and late paychecks as a lesser evil to the threat of layoffs and voluntary retirements, which were increasingly less voluntary. "Actually, many of the contracts approved by the Labor Ministry were not complied with. That is, the contract would be signed, and the money failed to appear. We would complain to the Ministry, but the official record of the contract had disappeared."

In Argentina, the layoff system was privatized to achieve greater efficiency. In this case, "efficiency" means using the "mutual agreement" between workers and employers as a disguise to lay off more employees, more easily. However, in this contract case, the records had disappeared. For Ojeda, the only explanation for this enigma is a fist pounded on the table: "Somebody must have laid down money."

Christmas with Pennies

You can always be worse off. Argentina realized this in 2001 when the Menem recession and its overlap with Fernando de la Rúa's administration brought on the absolute collapse of the economy. In that context, Gonzalo kept paying his workers less and less. From wages close to 1,000 pesos a month, he went on to pay fractions of 150 pesos a week, then 100, and finally, 50 pesos a week. While he was at it, he also humiliated the workers by making them wait up to seven hours outside of their shift to cash in those 50 pesos.

But at the same time, Gonzalo was expanding his businesses as owner and president of Conforguías Inc., where Conforti's clients and contracts would end. That's why the workers began to suspect that a new black magic act was unfolding before their eyes—whatever there was simply disappeared. They called it "emptying out." By the end of 2001 Conforti was left with a single client—the Spanish newspaper, El País, which has a small circulation in

Buenos Aires and Montevideo, Uruguay.

Raúl Gonzalo attended a creditors' meeting. "We kept working," Juan José Rodríguez recognizes, "and moreover, we worked
for free on Saturdays and Sundays. We did it thinking that it
would be even worse if the company closed down."

When the workers would hold assemblies to demand their
back wages, Gonzalo would go down to lecture them. Miguel
Isidro Barrios is still surprised by the arguments. "You know what
he would say to us? He said that the company's crisis was our fault.
He said that we did the work poorly and that was why the clients
would leave."

December 2001 arrived. *Corralito.*[2] Ojeda complains, "But the
corralito didn't affect this guy. He would go to Uruguay to get the
money." Nobody knows exactly how much, but on Christmas in
2001 he paid each of the workers ten pesos. At that point there
were around eighty workers, so Gonzalo invested 800 pesos for
their happy holidays. There is one strange fact—he paid them in
coins, because it was the only small change he could find.

Not everyone he owed got his or her ten coins. In addition to
the lapsed wages, the AFIP, other government agencies, social security, and the union created a debt that—like the Argentine foreign debt—was becoming increasingly unmanageable.

To avoid paying some of that debt, Gonzalo attempted a new
esoteric maneuver—he declared, under oath to the AFIP, that he
had no employees. He made them disappear into thin air.

However, he later petitioned the Labor Ministry to invoke a Crisis
Prevention Procedure so he could fire half of the workforce. In conclusion: he had no employees, but he was going to fire half of them.

This theory about the division of nothing deserved an arduous philosophical debate, the Nobel Prize for Physics, or restorations for the victims of an illicit association between this type of businessmen and a neoliberal state that supports them by providing them these services.

The Reactivation of Counterfeit

In late February 2003, the workers were fed up and began a so-called "work retention"—since they weren't getting paid, they would show up to work to do nothing. Regardless, they collaborated on what was essential for *El País* to continue being published. Gonzalo then announced that he was no longer able to pay

Schooling

There are already at least three reclaimed factories with operating middle schools on site: IMPA, Gráfica Patricios, and Maderera Córdoba. At IMPA there is a school for adults, specializing in cooperativism and micro-enterprises, administered by a cooperative of educators who had to organize themselves under the private education system in order to provide official degrees. With a completely different style, in Gráfica Patricios, the Buenos Aires Education Department opened a school specializing in graphic arts. It participates in the "Zero Desertion" program, whose objective is to reincorporate students who have dropped out of middle school. Simultaneously, in Maderera Córdoba, the Adult Education 2000 Plan is working to provide diplomas.

the workers even the 50 pesos a week that they had been cashing in and that a complete work suspension began on March 10th. The judge at the creditors' hearing, Juan José Dieuzeide, assigned the case a supervisor.

Gonzalo counterattacked by filing a lawsuit for "establishment occupation" and demanding the workers' evacuation. The factory was actually not taken nor occupied—the workers simply showed up for their shifts. Even the judicial supervisor himself presented the judge with a document describing that there was no such occupation. "The plant is controlled," he reported, "by the Libercoop security company and by additional personnel of the Argentine Federal Police, in permanent contact with Gonzalo himself."

There were more attempted magic tricks. Gonzalo claimed that his debt to the workers was insignificant and that he had paid them all their 2002 wages. To prove it, he did what was logical—he turned in all the receipts signed by the workers to the judicial supervisor.

There was only one troubling detail—all the signatures, in more than 300 receipts, were forged. At a glance, it was obvious that the same person appeared to have signed using radically different signatures, which the judge himself was able to confirm without having to overly scrutinize the chicken scratch. This is something that would spark indignation in any honest citizen, and even any efficient forger.

Private Justice

With the discovery of the counterfeit and everything else that it implied as criminal behavior, the arrest warrant was issued.

However, it wasn't for Raúl Gonzalo, but rather, for the workers accused of trespassing by Judge Mónica Atucha de Ares, of the

National Corrections Court #2. This woman demonstrated the speed that justice is sometimes capable of—sometimes—by accepting the trespassing complaint, ordering the evacuation of workers from a factory that they were not occupying, and issuing indictments against fourteen of the workers who were at the location on the day that she sent a judicial official to inspect.

The judge, in a situation similar to what occurred with the provincial judge Marcelo Goldberg in the Crometal case, placed the defense of private property and eviction above all other interests and rights. And she did this despite the fact that she was dealing with an elusive counterfeiter, accused of deliberately making the company go under. Judge Golderg ended up personally apologizing to the workers as soon as he realized he was opening himself up to a political trial. On the other hand, Judge Atucha de Ares continues holding the pending eviction threat.

Don Aniceto Sanabria, one of the cooperative's veterans, says out loud, "There's no justice here, right?" None of us who were with him at that moment had anything new to say.

The workers brought up the idea of an expropriation law that they borrowed from legislators in Buenos Aires.

Gustavo Ojeda recalls, "Our intention was to establish a graphic arts school, a health center for Barracas and La Boca, and a cultural center right here." It's the IMPA model, cloned by other cooperatives.

Ghelco Is Contagious

The idea to steer the conflict in the direction of a cooperative came from a comment that a police officer made to Gustavo. The officer told him, "Look, these people went through numerous problems and ended up establishing a cooperative and keeping the factory." The officer also gave him a telephone number. Consequently, Gustavo was able to contact Ghelco workers who were in charge of the Vieytes Worker Cooperative that manufactures products for coffee shops and ice cream parlors. Then Gustavo told his graphic union about the situation, and from there he was put in contact with Eduardo Murúa, from the National Movement of Reclaimed Companies.

When asked what effect this whole situation had on their families, the cooperative workers are sober. Ojeda says, "The families support us." But Cristófero Gramajo frowns as he says, "It was very hard."

The Silent Media

The conflict had an anorexic repercussion on the media. The oddest examples were Channel 9 and the newspaper *Página/ 12* (printed at Conforti until the mid-1990s), both of which wrote a piece on the conflict that was never aired nor published. Gustavo Ojeda says, "The *Página* people came to write an article about us, but we later discovered that it wasn't published because of the relationship that Gonzalo had with the newspaper's bosses."

The workers continued running into Gonzalo at the Labor Ministry. During one encounter, Gonzalo confessed the difficulties he was facing, including not being able to pay the insurance for his, or his wife's, 4x4. In any event, his decline below levels of automotive subsistence does not appear to have come to pass. Soon thereafter, the workers saw them both arrive at Conforti in their respective trucks. This should serve to calm the allies and friends of the family and the insurance salespeople.

The union (Buenos Aires Graphic Federation) financially supported the workers while they waited for the expropriation. (Before, the Chilavert workers had not received any support whatsoever.) "For me, it was a metamorphosis. I was a union delegate for nine years and then suddenly, I had to think that we all had to be owners of the company," says a surprised Ojeda.

Under the watch of Lauro Vázquez and Gustavo Mirando, two of the cooperative's youngest members (there were a few thirty-somethings, while the rest were older), Don Aniceto Sanabria takes the floor: "You have asked many questions. May I ask you one? Why is this Gonzalo guy not in prison? Is there any justice?"

In Early 2004, Everything Changed

The Patricios Graphic Worker Cooperative won the Temporary Expropriation Law for the workshop on February 27th, and the definitive expropriation on November 25th. There's no more graffiti. And, increasingly, the place rumbles with rotations. "We started little by little, but now we are working all week," says one of the workers. He smiles while one of his coworkers drives a motor cart that comes and goes between the machines with loads of magazines and brochures. They no longer play cards—they don't have to kill time anymore. The soul of the place has changed.

Patricios Graphics has twenty-eight members, but there are already six more candidates who are working there day to day. "The idea is that as the volume of work increases, they will definitely be brought on full time," says Ojeda, who operates the machines on the night shift.

Their customers came back. Some of them include: Poligráfica del Plata for the printing of magazines like *Mía* and *Debate* and the brochures for Auchan supermarkets (in this case alone, they are producing a circulation of 400,000 copies), products like *Enfoques Alternativos* (of the Communist Party), *El Vocero Boliviano, El Descamisado*, neighborhood magazines, and subcontracted work from publishers like Perfil.

"You have to recall that this is where the newspapers *Página/12, El Cronista Comercial,* and the local printing of the Spanish paper *El País* were carried out," Ojeda reminds, in order to explain the print shop's potential.

They started out taking home 100 pesos a week per worker. They're already up to 200, with the goal of reaching 1,000 pesos a month. "And then, we'll create different job titles," Ojeda proposes, considering that they all charge the same amount now, but supposing that in due time they will have to recognize different responsibility levels. "If not, coworkers get lazy. I'll come in later, or not show up, since I still get paid the same."

The cooperative's dream is to have 200 to 250 workers again, taking full advantage of its potential.

Gustavo, who was a union delegate for ten years leading up to the conflict, is not falsely optimistic about the reclaimed factory movement's potential to be contagious. "The issue is to raise the consciousness of the workers in order to bring them into the struggle. But the truth is that it's very hard, very intense. Many times, the workers simply want to go to work, get paid, and go home."

But even in those cases, what would the workers prefer, if they had the choice? Would they choose to work under a boss (private or governmental) or do what they are doing now? "The people here now won't ever leave. But those who don't know what working in a cooperative is like might prefer to continue as they are and disassociate themselves from the problems. That's why it's good for them to know what things are like in a cooperative."

Other News

The Buenos Aires Education Department opened a school specializing in graphic skills at the plant, as part of a program to reincorporate youth who have dropped out of school. There are already 140 students between the ages of 15 and 19 studying there.

The Barracas Library and its 30,000 volumes have also moved into the plant.

There is also a cultural center up and running, with lessons on everything from dance and theater to chess, and festivals every weekend.

They plan to establish an after-school center for the neighborhood's children and a health clinic. These are all proposals, but keeping in mind the success they've had with each of their initiatives so far, the cooperative has gained credit.

Gustavo says, "I'm very enthusiastic about this whole project. A few years ago, thinking about reclaiming a factory was utopian. Sincerely, I think this is historic for the workers' movement."

In terms of the daily grind, he observes how the work environment has changed, "We're all much more relaxed, calm, and without fear of reprisals. That generates more responsibility. At the same time, we have to raise our coworkers' consciousness for everyone to understand that we have to defend each job and demonstrate that we can manage the company better than anyone else."

They do it every day. Gustavo likens it to tiny battles won within a larger conflict between two opposing forces: "There are guys who wake up in the morning thinking about how to screw people, and others who think about how to rebuild this Argentina that has been torn apart."

Chapter Seven

Renacer

An Explosion at the End of the World

The ex-Aurora Corporation, expropriated and now in the hands of the Renacer Cooperative, waged a battle that lasted several years— enduring pickets at -14°C (7°F), disputes with the Metallurgical Workers' Union (UOM), and opposing political power. People who simply wanted to work found themselves obligated to take back the factory by force, to occupy the Banco Nación, the Legislature, and the provincial government itself. Follow along with the details of a shocking story, the curse of a crisis, and uncertainties about the future.

Margarita Monla is from the province of San Juan. Nobody would guess that her oldest son is twenty-one-years-old. She is a woman who projects serenity, and it doesn't seem wise to make her lose it. After all, she managed to lead a factory into revolt.

Monica Acosta, even younger, barely in her thirties, is still losing her Cordoban accent ten years after moving south to Ushuaia, and has attained an unreachable utopia that models

dream of—she's not just a pretty face, as the UOM members that
expelled her from the union can testify. They expelled her for defending the workers. Their decision can be called reactionary, sex-
ist, bureaucratic, and ugly. But they weren't able to kick her out of
the factory, which she and her coworkers ended up reclaiming—
sweeping the UOM out with the dust.

Drunkenness and Downfall

The story begins in 1996, in the Menem era, when the Aurora
home appliances factory closed all its plants, including the one in
Ushuaia with 750 workers. A combination of dollar-peso parity,
impossible competition from will-nilly importing, and the Tequila
Effect (the neoliberal hangover from the 1995 financial binge and
collapse of the Mexican currency) sunk the company. It did not
sink the owners—the Tarsiuks—who, according to Monica, con-
jured up a fraudulent bankruptcy, emigrated to other businesses
and safeguarded their money in foreign countries far from this
cold climate. "But the national and provincial governments and
the UOM wanted to avoid the social explosion that appeared to be
on the verge of breaking out at any moment—for example, they
killed Víctor Choque.[1] So they proposed self-management of the
factory by Renacer Incorporated, and the provincial government
provided 1,800,000 pesos as start-up capital."

Facing the precipice of unemployment, the workers accepted
this option. They all formed part of the corporation, thinking that
working with the UOM itself would guarantee that things would
go in the right direction. "There was a bond of trust, they had
been there through the workers' struggles."

Soon thereafter, the corporation's board of directors, formed by the UOM leaders, began to talk in doublespeak. "They sounded more and more like the old bosses, there were constant contradictions, but everything was laid bare by the wages."

The hard truth: in this factory—a workplace where all were "compañeros"—the workers made 500 pesos a month, and those on the board of directors made over 5,000. Also worth noting: the UOM's general secretary, Marcelo Sosa, was also the corporation's president.

The efficiency of this sort of UOM-run corporation that Renacer had become was striking—in a short time, they had accumulated an inexplicable 700,000-peso debt. The directors called a general meeting and, seeming nervous, informed them that everyone would have to make a sacrifice to save their jobs. Each would have to take a $5,000 personal loan from the Banco de Tierra del Fuego.

This time the directors chose to practice democratic equality—the workers who made 500 pesos and the big shots who made $5,000 all had to borrow exactly the same.

Cash for the Politicians

The year 2000 was well under way. Margarita and Monica tell how UOM Incorporated also spent fortunes paying their loyal supporters for overtime they didn't work. "The body of delegates[2] was like the mafia—whoever complained started receiving threatening phone calls. They even stoned some union members' houses." That was the price paid by those who suspected that the egalitarian democracy of the union leaders was not exactly wise.

The ratio in the delegates council was 13 to 2: 13 UOM Incorporated officers and two nonmembers, one of whom was Monica herself, who belonged to the union, but did not toe the line.

This was resolved predictably—they kicked her out of the UOM. They weren't able to expel her from the factory, but they cut off her union privileges. She went back to the production line, but she was transferred from the washing machine packaging section—where she had previously worked, and was in day-to-day contact with her coworkers—to a button-pushing job that was located in a dark room, kind of like an attic. "It was the worst, because all my coworkers came to see me anyway, and that made them even more angry."

While Monica Acosta's expulsion was being cooked up, the UOM Corporation sent Margarita Monla a pink slip. The factory had suspended 70 percent of the workforce for sixty-eight days, but the media reported that it was only for a month. On top of this, it was discovered that the company was still receiving extravagant loans, on the order of 150,000 pesos, from the National Treasury (ATN). Margarita denounced both situations on television, so they fired her using a quite creative telegram. In it the UOM accused her of damaging the company's image. Margarita holds out her hands wide apart, "The notice was this big. It was like a proclamation."

Until then, the conflicts at the company had been sporadic, "Monica and I hadn't joined forces. She protested on one side and I, who worked in the television section, had gone to the press. When they fired me, everyone was opposed. I never missed work. I hadn't stolen. Why were they firing me? For telling the truth? My compañeros and I went together to the UOM, where they were deliberating Monica's expulsion from the union. But what united us the most was that, instead of fighting her own expulsion, she was there fighting to get me rehired."

Now united, they moved from the UOM to the factory, and occupied the board of directors' offices. "That forced the board of directors to rehire Marga," Monica explains. The next day the monstrous pink slip was worthless.

At the same time, the company was falling apart, and news broke that it had run up a debt of more than 20 million pesos with the backing of the provincial government led by Carlos Manfredotti. Marcelo Sosa and other members of the board of directors resigned, in what was the beginning of a plan to close the factory. Once they resigned, the government gave many of the trade unionists government jobs. One suspicion is that the giant debt had served, among other possible bankrolls, to finance incumbents' political campaigns.

Monica surmises, "He resigned to avoid paying the price for the factory's closing, but he continued pulling all the strings from the above. It was Sanyo who wanted to buy Renacer." Rumor had it that the sale would keep the plant open, but with only 150 jobs.

The Ax

At that point in the year 2000, about 400 workers had stuck it out at the plant. The Comisión de Lucha (literally "Struggle Commission") was formed, and Monica, the expelled unionist, was unanimously elected to it.

In March of 2001 the factory doors were closed. UOM Incorporated and the Labor Ministry agreed on a "crisis prevention" measure—the factory was to be closed to the workers for three

months. Monica continues, "Since they took away the possibility
of fighting from the inside—something that is key in these struggles—we pitched a tent outside, ready to stay until the end of the
lockout period."

Readers should be aware that we are talking about temperatures between -10° and 10°C (14–50°F, during the warmer days of
that season). Cold, freezing rain, and snow. Solution: trashcan fires
in the middle of the tent, to warm up at least a little bit. To keep
up a 24-hour presence, they took turns staying in the tent. Other
than their mere presence, their objective was to keep any materials
or machinery from disappearing from the plant. They couldn't go
in, but none of what was inside could get out.

The UOM members pushed for the sale of the factory, "Some
coworkers weren't supporting it, out of bad intentions, but
thought that it was best to sell and at least save a hundred [jobs].
We said, 'No one will be left out.' " Monica says that those who
wanted to sell were pitted against those who wanted to hold out.

Once the "crisis prevention" time period was up, on June 8, all
the workers met around the tent at 4 a.m. to decide what to do at
six, when the first shift began.

The question that night around the tent was: What do we do?
"We had two possibilities," Monica says, "we either waited for the
bureaucratic solution and petitioned the Labor Ministry, or we
went the workers' route and entered the factory directly."

Petitioning the authorities wasn't very promising. The workers
had filed a lawsuit against the government for fraud, and for its
complicity in the stripping of the company.

The other option, of simply going in without much discussion, struck fear into everyone. There was a private security guard at the plant and no one ruled out the possibility of governmental repression.

In the face of cold and fear, it's advisable to move. Everything was done quite calmly—one of the workers took the initiative, and along with it, an ax. A group mostly made up of women followed him in.

When the police arrived, responding to a report of trespassing, they found the door in perfect shape, a brand-new lock, and a fresh coat of paint. "The workers had fixed everything in a flash. And the police officer who was going to perform the inventory had the bright idea of writing his report using a surface with fresh paint to write on." The police officer decided to write his report on his paint-stained paper, saying everything was perfectly normal. Monica said, "They were outnumbered. There were a ton of us and they had sent a few cops as cannon fodder."

Like a Cat in a Bag

Since they had pitched the tent, and even more so once they reentered the still-dormant factory, the Comisión de Lucha's job was that of an unemployed workers movement—to provide for the needs of workers and their families in a situation that Marga describes as dismal.

Inside the factory, the administration remained in the hands of a pro-bureaucratic group. Margarita remembers, "We had everything against us, workers in their forties and over, a slander campaign and media that acted—almost entirely—in favor of the government and the union bureaucracy. The local community was divided—many didn't want to defend the factory."

They tallied up their supporters: public sector—zero; unions—less than zero; judicial—zero; media—zero.

The struggle was still against the UOM and what Monica describes as the "fake board of directors." There was electricity at the plant, but no gas. It was impossible to get the factory running, and 2,000 liters of paint from the electrocoating sector had been lost. Monica notes, "They wanted to kill the factory in order to sell it and, in the process, destroy all the evidence of the black box that financed political campaigns, and the rest of the shenanigans they had committed."

They also had to come up with strategies to avoid utility cut-offs at the homes of the workers whose personal property was being seized to pay for the personal loans they had taken at the request of the union bosses. "Those hypocrites," Monica says indignantly, "hadn't paid a single peso, but they were going after us. We won that fight as well."

With the same determination, the workers asked the nearby university School of Engineering to study the company's viability, dealt with the Ansés (state retirement agency) in order to obtain subsidies, visited bankruptcy court, blocked roads in -14°C temperatures, met with authorities of Banco Nación, and occupied the bank when they needed to. They carried out a fundraising campaign called "one peso at a time" in order to turn the gas back on in the factory.

Time and perseverance began to play in their favor. They increasingly won support for a nerve-racking, unfair struggle to reclaim their jobs in a factory that was empty and comatose. This is how the years 2001 and 2002 went by for the workers, until two members of the board of directors resigned and the trustee, who was sympathetic to the workers, named two replacements. One was Margarita Monla. Control over the factory was no longer solely in the hands of the union group, which had prudently begun their retreat.

The idea was to not slow down. "We took some bold measures, but we never went too far. We occupied the government building. First two of us walked in to make an appointment, and behind them we all went in. We weren't screwing around. We knew they could beat us like a cat in a bag. But at the same time, we weren't dumb. We sought a dialogue with government or judicial officials, and we knew that without the support of nationwide organizations like the CTA[3] or the National Movement of Reclaimed Factories, they would have swept us aside. We were in a feudal province, where Manfredotti hadn't faced a single strike in four years as governor."

The Expropriation

The idea of a cooperative had been brewing for a long time. "We weren't opposed to any solution, but expropriation seemed like the best option. We formed the cooperative with the condition of equal wages, making basic decisions by assembly. We are against the division of manual and intellectual work, we want a rotation of positions and, above all, the ability to recall our elected leaders."

The expropriation of Renacer became the principal issue in the province's elections. When Manfredotti lost the race for governor, the workers received some incredible news—the UOM had declared itself in favor of the expropriation. "Now we can surely rest easy," was how the workers reacted to such support.

In the legislature, indecision ruled. Some representatives told them, "This goes against private property; they're going to cook us all." The workers visited the judge that oversaw bankruptcy. The response: "The only way I'm not going to order everything to be auctioned off is by expropriating the plant. I'm not going to go through a political trial to delay that."

The legislators proposed waiting until August. On July 13, 2003, they were to set a date for the debate. That's when the crowd showed up.

Marga relates, "Teachers, municipal employees, taxi drivers, neighbors, family members came. It was beautiful. When those guys said that it was best to further examine the issue at a later time, we began to pick our spots on the carpet to spend the night. On July 14th it was one in the morning and we didn't let anyone leave. We weren't leaving and they weren't going to leave either."

Monica continues, "If we hadn't put our foot down, surely the next day there wouldn't have been a session. They wanted to suspend it, but the next day they were all super nice."

The workers relaxed a bit when they considered what Marga observed, "If they vote against us, at least we have them all together and we can tear their hair out right there on the spot." She kept up a dialogue with one legislator. She was persuasive, and the legislators ended up improving the proposed bill in favor of the workers and ceding the building and machines to the Renacer Cooperative. The vote was twelve in favor, with only three abstentions.

Mysterious Ending

With the materials they had at the plant and plenty of ingenuity, they managed to build 120 washing machines that they sold in Ushuaia for 650 pesos. With that capital they restored several parts of the plant and have managed to put together 300 more, whose sale they were negotiating with the home appliance store chain Easy before the provincial government ended up buying them. Margarita says, from her own experience and from what people have told her, that these are the kind of washing machines that get passed down from mother to daughter, generation to generation. "They last no fewer than eight or ten years, they are really high quality, and at better prices than the imported ones, and we make the spare parts ourselves."

If everything goes well, the factory will be able to revive several lines of home appliances.

They also seem to be able to resuscitate a few dreams, like those of 90 percent of Ushuaia and Río Grande's factories that collapsed in the neoliberal earthquake. Some now feel that the solution found by the ex-Aurora company can be a solution for them as well.

Monica never had many illusions about Kirchner's government, not even in his post-electoral honeymoon, at his highest level of popularity, "The people aren't stupid. There are a bunch of issues that seem very attractive and high-minded, but the main problem continues to be hunger and the 20 million Argentines living in poverty. That hasn't been addressed. The children are worse off. The elderly are worse off—there isn't a single improvement. How many factories has Kirchner reopened since he took over?"

Monica says that with the cooperative running (in which neither she nor Margarita hold a leadership position, since they continue in the Comisión de Lucha), what they want to avoid is "regressing." She's talking about the kind of attitudes they had to put up with from the UOM unionists. "We don't want any more disloyal unions. We have to reclaim the companies, but also the unions." She proposes something that would sound strange in many unions: "The union representatives should work."

In 2003 President Nestor Kirchner signed the Industrial Promotion Law in favor of Renacer, in the presence of members of the factory's Comisión de Lucha and the Class and Combative Current (CCC),[4] an organization to which Monica and Margarita belong. The photo of the president with the CCC's leader, Juan Carlos Alderete, was all over the media. Furthermore, the provincial government bought a total of 1,000 washing machines.

A year later the factory was still practically paralyzed and Monica Acosta calls the president "an enemy of the reclaimed companies," denouncing him for the fact that "he never made good on his promise to grant Renacer a loan of 900,000 pesos as start-up capital." Without capital it is impossible to purchase imported materials needed to reactivate the factory and to launch production. The CCC and Revolutionary Communist Party (the Maoist party that leads the CCC) publications report that the cooperative is "on the war path" after tasting the government's bitter broken promises.

At times it seems like the plant's crisis is a curse of metal and ice, from which no one can escape.

Time, and who knows how many struggles, will determine whether "renacer" (Spanish for "to be born again") is a beautiful concept that, in this case, only became a failed metaphor, or if it describes a project capable of living up to its name.

Chapter Eight

IMECC
The Tire Prophecy

The IMECC Clinic, peacefully occupied by its workers, was forcefully evacuated on March 12, 2004, using violent police repression (clubs, several wounded and one arrest by the riot squad). The workers responded by blocking Díaz Vélez Avenue in the Parque Centenario neighborhood of Buenos Aires. The government only intervened when it smelled the burning tires. The following is an eyewitness account of the eviction. The purpose of reproducing it here exactly as it was published on lavaca.org hours after it occurred—in the midst of rapidly changing events that required quick dissemination of the news—is to give a testimony of the repression that those who create and defend their own jobs face.

Elsa Montero's prophecy was fulfilled exactly as she had imagined it:

"In this country, they talk a lot about an increase in jobs, but it's the other way around—here you have to block roads and burn tires to make yourself heard."

The workers had peacefully occupied the six-story building of the Institute for Cardiovascular Medicine and Surgery (IMECC), a clinic providing highly specialized cardiovascular treatment. They were waiting for a decision to come through—Judge Matilde Ballerini (the same judge who carried out the expulsions at Brukman) did not want to give the property to the cooperative.

It was not about a winning lottery ticket for the workers. The cooperative's proposal was to buy the bankrupt clinic for one million dollars, paying it over five years in 43,000-peso monthly installments after renting it for a year. It should be said that the cooperative's was the only offer to buy the clinic (located on the corner of Díaz Velez and Otamendi Avenues in Buenos Aires) on the table.

The judge rejected the offer anyway, stating publicly that she would only accept turning it over to the city government in exchange for rent. It was already stipulated that those payments would be for 4,000 pesos per month, and that the cooperative would take charge of the clinic in exchange for compensation in medical services.

But that verbal agreement ran into two roadblocks: the governmental bureaucracy, which, after approving the project through its Health Ministry, did not establish a procedure for payment. (Is this kind of delay a mistake, or a strategy?) Secondly, the judge's unprecedented activism: after doing nothing for months, she ordered the workers' expulsion overnight, knowing that the government had a proposal on the table. (Is this kind of accelerated action a mistake, or a strategy?)

The executive and judicial powers thus ended up united by one thing: the victims of their actions and inactions.

The police—in armored vehicles, bulletproof vests, and riot gear—arrived at the clinic at 2 p.m. on Friday. They were watched over from above—a federal police helicopter seemed to be hanging from a cloud, similar to when trying to pacify a soccer riot.

The forces of order were to retake the clinic, which at the time was occupied by four people, two of them women. Two others had gone out to buy sodas to accompany their lunch of a roast chicken, donated by the National Movement of Reclaimed Companies (MNER) and cooked in the clinic's kitchen.

The police arrived with the trustee Eduardo Echaire, who had the key to the lock to remove the chains on the main entrance.

The paradox: Echaire had on paper stated that he was in favor of the clinic's staying open under worker control, but now he opened the lock to throw them out.

"What happens is that, as a trustee, he is obliged to obey the judge's order"—explains MNER lawyer Florencia Kravetz.

"Obedience to the judicial system?"

"Something like that."

Struggle and *El Chavo*

One worker let out a shout that never goes out of style: "The cops!"

Too late. The police were already inside. Liz, one of the clinic's workers, fled up the stairs to alert another coworker and to sound the alarm to the outside world by phone. A policeman chased her.

"He shouted for me to freeze, he screamed at me to stop, then he slipped and fell. Now that I think about it, it's hilarious. I kept running upstairs, but he caught up to me on the third floor and grabbed me by the hair. I told him to get out and to go grab... his mother's hair. (Liz is embarrassed now to repeat her own words.) One cop grabbed each of my arms and they shoved me all the way downstairs. In the lobby they were mistreating my coworkers.

I asked the guy, "And why are you doing all this?" "We're just doing our job," said one officer. "Well, that's what we want, to work," I told him. "Because if you steal, you know, you also go to jail and out through the back door. But someone who wants to work, who has a family and kids, in that case they don't even care. They do this to you."

Once the dangerous Liz was subdued, on the ground floor four policemen dedicated themselves exclusively to Hernán González, one of the two who had gone to buy sodas. Liz remembers, "They cornered him. They threw him on the floor. He defended himself. They pressed him against the wall with their clubs. And he kept struggling."

Hernán doesn't work at the clinic, he belongs to the Pompeya Neighborhood Assembly, and is the son of a worker at the reclaimed Chilavert Graphic Design Cooperative. Hernán's testimony is an X-ray of today's situation. "When I came back from buying the sodas I saw the police inside, and I felt so powerless that I just ran into the clinic. The commissioner said we were welcome to leave quietly, or he would have to use force."

"My compañeros said no. I said that we were convinced of what we were doing. They grabbed one of my arms, the other arm, then my legs. I was screaming all kinds of stuff at them.

"This is what you're going to leave for your grandchildren, goddamned son of a bitch?"

These sons of bitches continued their work by hauling
Hernán outside, "They threw me on the floor. They mopped the
sidewalk with me a little bit. One of their boots stepped on my
head, then on my neck. Another cop stepped on my ankle, which
still hurts. I don't even know at what point they injured my arm
(he points to the marks). In any case, later on a court doctor
signed a statement saying that I was in perfect shape."

Hernán was handcuffed, pushed into a police car and taken to
the 11th District police station. "In the police car I was screaming,
'My country or my life!' "

He laughs as he tells the story. During the occupation,
Hernán was one of the participants in the development of a Plan
A ("they give us the clinic peacefully") and a Plan B ("To run like
crazy screaming 'my country or my life!' ") that were written using
butcher paper on a wooden easel.

"At the police station they treated me like a gentleman. But we
still had arguments there.

They would say, 'Why don't you stop screwing around, man,
causing problems when you don't even work there?' I told them
about Chilavert's experience, where my old man works. I told them
that we don't want to fight with them, or to break the law. But sometimes the laws are unjust. Then we started debating about legitimacy
and legality. One said that the top police officials actually don't care
about these cops that they send to expel workers. They send them as
cannon fodder and then negotiate through other channels."

Hernán reports that he was treated cordially, "They left me
sitting at a table watching TV. [The famous old Mexican sitcom]
El Chavo was on."

A while later Florencia Kravetz arrived to bail him out. The commissioner said, "the guy resisted arrest," to justify Hernán's detention, who was in the next room watching the effects of Don Ramón's scolding of Chilindrina [characters on *El Chavo*]. Kravetz answered, "I would have resisted too. I think the problem is that being young in this country is dangerous. And so is working. When they closed the clinic last December 30th, I crossed the street and there were some guys at Centenario Park snorting cocaine next to some kids who were playing. I thought—what a shitty country—you can use drugs next to a bunch of kids, you can steal, do whatever you want, but you can't work."

Traffic Report

When Hernán was arrested, the police also attacked the first MNER members arriving at the scene, led by Eduardo Murúa (MNER's president) himself, who were trying to reoccupy the building. The riot police began to club the protesters, bloodying Sebastián Maiza's forehead.

"I work at IMPA. They called to tell us about the expulsion at the clinic and we came. The cops were at the door. They had already arrested one worker (Hernán). The deal was that we were outside. At one point we decided to try and get in through a side door to retake the clinic. The cops were at the front door. They started clubbing us. It was totally pointless. Murúa had already managed to get in, but they forced him out. An ambulance came and treated me. Well, they just cleaned my head off. It's going to need stitches," said Maiza, awhile after the attack, wearing a bloodied shirt and a bandage on his head.

Hernán and Florencia returned to the clinic, where more and more workers from other reclaimed factories were rallying. They had already formed roadblocks on Díaz Vélez Avenue, as well as the streets Malvinas Argentinas and Otamendi. They piled up old tires, wood, and styrofoam mattresses, all soaked in kerosene and ready to be lit.

The people who organized these barricades were not those piqueteros with a frightening look about them, whom the mass media play up to excite people who demand order and toughness on crime. These people were ordinary workers. They weren't wearing masks. Some were even wearing suits. But their patience had run out, and they stood ready with their lighters drawn.

The tires began to burn. Parque Centenario was engulfed in a strange-smelling black cloud. The news spread quickly over the radio during the segment that usually covers these kinds of conflicts—the traffic report.

Diego Kravetz, a Kirchnerist Buenos Aires legislator, also an MNER lawyer like his sister Florencia, was trying to wear each of those hats. Sleeves rolled up, his tie loosened around his neck, he was talking on a silver cellphone in the middle of a column of dark smoke. At that point everyone assumed that someone from the government would take charge of the situation. Diego believed that the judge was not going to leave things as they were after ordering the expulsion and unleashing a social conflict. "Nobody manages to become a judge by being stupid," he said. Subsequent judicial actions tried to prove him wrong.

Actually, there wasn't stupidity involved, but his diagnosis was right regarding an ideological stubbornness of a judge who would try anything—except a solution that benefited the workers.

Those Who Were Not There

The flames were rising. Kravetz looked on, worried. There weren't many people at those jammed intersections—maybe 150. Perhaps what was most interesting was who *wasn't* there:

The union leaders, who tend to stay away from issues like defending jobs, weren't there. In a way, the workers won long-awaited unity among the unions: there were no *gordos* (fat, lazy bureaucrats) nor any *combativos* (combative unionists), neither CGT nor CTA.[1]

The leftist and/or progressive (we leave the strict definitions of these terms in readers' hands) Kirchnerist legislators weren't there. Many had signed pledges to support the workers, but, with few exceptions, stayed away from the clubs and flames.

The leftist parties weren't there. They show a certain disdain for the cooperatives, which they consider to not be revolutionary or "conscious" enough (lacking the consciousness not provided to them by the leftist parties).

There were no members from what can now be called the piquetero establishment, which does not participate in this kind of struggle.

There were no political academics, sociologists, political philosophers, social researchers, or any other academics, who perhaps, like the legislators, don't work on Friday afternoons or have more interesting issues to study.

Nor were there any government functionaries who postulate that this is a serious country in which we need to create real jobs.

Neither were the human rights organizations, many of whom have been absorbed lately in historical debates belonging in a museum.[2]

The relationship of numbers compared to strength is hard to measure, so it was difficult to say if these absences represented a weakness or a strength for the people tending the flames, with one eye on the helicopter hovering overhead. A federal police truck tried to bust through the roadblock on Díaz Vélez. It couldn't—so it backed up and tried through Otamendi. The MNER workers stood bare-chested in the truck's way. Hernán González had already forgotten about *El Chavo*—he sat down on the asphalt in front of the vehicle, which was forced to stop in order to avoid running people over. Some workers wanted to drag the officers out of their truck and give them the same treatment they had earlier received. Meanwhile, the riot squad looked

Getting Away with Murder

During demonstrations by social movements, the state's repressive forces have committed crimes that remain unpunished. Among them are the deaths of:

• Teresa Rodríguez, in Cutral Có, Neuquén (April 1997).
• Anibal Verón in Mosconi (November 2000).[3]
• Carlos Santillán and Omar Barrios, in Mosconi (June 2001). The same police attack left 80 injured, among them Iván Dorado, 19, who was left paraplegic.
• During the rebellion of December 19-20, 2001 (i.e. the *Argentinazo*), the government declared a state of siege. Around the country, 33 people were killed and 4,500 were arrested.
• On June 26, 2002, police killed Dario Santillán and Maximiliano Kosteki in an attack at the Avellaneda Bridge in Buenos Aires.

on from the other side of the flames. The truck decided that it had to back off. The workers began to jump up and down, chanting at the riot police a song that recalled another historical event. *Que se vayan todos, que no quede uno solo.*

Provocations

Police stood, arms crossed, at the front door of the clinic. The workers sat holding a *Fénix Salud* [the name of the reclaimed clinic, "Phoenix Health"] flag. Speaking over the drums, Florencia Kravetz talked about the police:

When you talk to them, 80 percent say they agree with the workers. I don't think they're lying to me. They realize that they are being thrown into a fight that pits poor against poor. But the orders are given, and without giving it a second thought, they repress the poor people right next to them ... people who are just like them.

Again, respecting the system.

But I don't want to believe that. I never did, really. But it's sad—you feel like an idiot. They tell you, "I agree with you," and then they repress you. Just like there were women cops who acted correctly, the ones outside, I saw how the cops inside were looking for a fight. I saw how they provoked the workers, "son of a bitch, go on, come over here" they were screaming, provoking the workers so they could attack them.

And the government's attitude?

I'm really disappointed. The official statements are very nice—but since there's no action behind their words, it has left me, as a young person participating in a social movement, personally, very disillusioned. The governmental organisms demand guarantees from the workers that are impossible to comply with, that not even the banks ask for. They announce credit opportunities, but they don't implement the measures to make it happen. There is absolute silence in respect to workers' needs. If you have a double-digit unemployment rate and a paralyzed production system, it doesn't matter how many speeches you give. You still don't have industry. And without industry, you don't have a real country. It's a country without a future.

Eduardo Murúa, a few steps away, chimed in.

"As always, there is an international division of labor. Argentina has to produce soy and natural resources for other countries. That's all. To make it worse, those products don't generate jobs, but instead, exclusion, unemployment, and economic concentration. That's the current policy."

A group of twenty men were jumping and screaming, "IMECC belongs to the workers and if you don't like it, screw you, screw you." And yelling at the police, "Hey what's the matter you pig? / you look pretty pissed off / they don't pay you squat / but you still defend them."[4]

Rumors spread that negotiations between the judge and government functionaries were in progress. Not with the Buenos Aires city government (where the clinic is located), nor the Labor Ministry. The talks were established with the Justice Ministry.

How could the situation on that corner be explained politically? Murúa, drinking *mate* and smoking, sitting on the steps of the clinic guarded by the federal police, offers an atypical analysis for those times. "There is an ideological advance by the Right, and there are no political sectors interested in the workers' struggle.

Judge Ballerini's decision is cold and calculated. It intends to cause a social conflict because she is convinced, along with other segments of the Right, that workers should not control businesses. The Right is arguing through the newspapers that social programs [unemployment benefits] are more important than workers reclaiming genuine work. And the government does the same as the Right. The subsidy is there, the deceptive plans like Manos a la Obra are there.[5] We don't attack them or oppose them, but they're not real jobs. The truth is that the government has no policy to deal with this issue."

Defending the Creditor

What is Murúa referring to? On March 4, 2004, *La Nación* published an editorial called "The dilemma of the occupied factories." It proposes that it is "highly probable" that the number of companies in this condition will grow, that judges cannot avoid the situation, and will have to find some way to resolve the conflicts. "For this same reason the acts of trespassing go unpunished. After the worker expulsion at Brukmann [the double "n", as if the surname was German, is a typical anti-Semitic lapse] force has practically not been used to take back the occupied plants," the newspaper speculates.

Using the phrase "it is estimated" the newspaper points to an expenditure of 60 million pesos supposedly spent on reclaimed companies. This information is public and well known, making their statistic a lie (a lie allowing the editorialist to continue his monologue).

It later suggests that one aspect that makes the capitalist system work is that new firms replace obsolete ones that go bankrupt.

So, an adequate bankruptcy law is one that allows for "assets to be acquired by new and more efficient businessmen, to get production started again." Businessmen—not cooperatives.

The editorial continues: "By the same token, selling off assets should lead to alternative uses for the buildings and for the scrapping of machinery if they no longer have any value as a functioning enterprise. This is the 'creative destruction' that Joseph Schumpeter described in his theory on economic development."

The article thus arrives at the fallacy that reclaimed companies are not viable (which is refuted by their very existence) and one unforgettable sentence reads, "It is preferable to spend public money to subsidize unemployment or on other civic projects."

Therefore, although "not a single damned peso"—as Murúa would say—has been spent on these companies, if there was money, it would be better spent on unemployment benefits, and keeping the unemployed as hostages of the state or welfare organizations.

La Nación continues, "These unnecessary things are even less appropriate in times when our government is faced with the challenge of getting out of default and is not achieving a sufficient initial surplus to propose payment conditions acceptable to its creditors." The interests the newspaper favors are evident.

There's more. "There are no criticisms from foreign creditors or other governments of the heavy spending on social plans that are today alleviating a grave employment and food emergency. On the other hand, they do object to unnecessary or pointless expenditures that, in some cases, are simply politically motivated."

Translation: maintaining subsidies and welfare is consistent with what foreign creditors demand. Recovering genuine employment, on the other hand, is "pointless" and simply politically motivated. What is economically healthy is paying the creditors.

The sermon concludes by saying that the justice system should change its mind before allowing for the continuation of bankrupt and "apparently nonviable" companies, and prioritize the competitive sale of assets to "competent and experienced" businessmen (one should remember those competent and experienced individuals who stripped these companies of their assets and plunged them into bankruptcy) or "worker cooperatives, taking care that these groups do not become privileged benefactors of the state."

From what one gathers from this warning, the ones who should be the benefactors of the state are the creditors.

The MNER sent a copy of this editorial to government representatives, senators, and legislators of Buenos Aires so that they would publicly define their position on the issue. Guillermo Robledo of MNER explains, "There is a fundamental fight against the system here. The system doesn't tolerate workers taking charge of the companies' continued existence. It needs to scrap these companies, not for the workers to get them back on their feet. This is what the *La Nación* editorial proves. So we're going to propose a very simple system to the whole Argentine political establishment. Just as there is an economic emergency decree, that emergency decree should be extended so judges can't choose to expel workers and scrap the factories. They should give them an opportunity to have three years to keep them alive. Of course this would break down the lucrative business of asset sales benefiting the judges, trustees, and the rest. It's a tough proposal because it says that the right to private property has a limit—it's not exercised unconditionally. The right to work comes first. It's a fundamental ideological debate."

Time will tell if this debate is fundamental or not, and how it is resolved. Murúa, on the IMECC steps, describes the unfolding political and economic environment, and his position with respect to the criminalization of protest, "Politicians can't bring themselves to speak out against us, but they also don't do anything to ease the pressure on the workers from the Right and the judges. We always hear promises, and nothing more than promises. There is no public policy. What's more, they made a big deal in an appearance with the president in December trying to get recovered companies together—we didn't attend—saying that loans would be available. We still haven't seen a single goddamned peso. They subsidize the big corporations and monopolies, that's for sure."

"We already told Kirchner himself," he continues, "that we won't negotiate with a president at the Casa Rosada (the presidential residence) while there are still criminal charges pending against a bunch of compañeros who fought against this economic model. If the government says that it wants to change politics and is seriously against the previous [economic and social] model, it can't threaten to prosecute those who fought against that model. There should be an immediate amnesty. I'm not disappointed with the government. I don't believe that a government can be the people's government despite staying in the hands of the same people who have governed for the last twenty years. I don't believe in a popular government that doesn't call on its citizens to participate in making the most important decisions. Democracy, as it's proposed today, doesn't serve the people. We need to find mechanisms of direct democracy. The people are mature enough for that. The time has passed when a few decide for the multitude—now we want everyone to decide."

Who Eats the Chicken

Night was falling when the news arrived: a compromise had been reached. The judge had named the National Secretary for Human Rights as trustee of the clinic and withdrew the police. There was a standing ovation, hugs, tears. Elsa Montero hugs Murúa. Hernán hugs his father, Cándido, and more chants break out, "And now you see, today we beat them once again," the classic *"El pueblo, unido, jamás será vencido"* (The people, united, shall never be defeated), "What fools, now they can stick the expulsion [order] up their asses," and "Look, look, take a photo, now they retreat to the 11th [police station] with their tails between their legs."[6]

Florencia Kravetz: "They hand over legal possession to the secretary, Eduardo Duhalde. The *good* Duhalde," she says, using her fingers to indicate quotation marks around her last two words. "Duhalde names a worker commission to oversee the assets, open the clinic, and continue the reclaiming process."

"The truth is that the workers don't even want expropriation. They don't want anything from the state—they want to buy the clinic because they consider it a profitable enterprise. Actually, they would be giving the state a source of employment, health services, and tax payments. This is the state's first gesture. I dismiss it, but it's a strong gesture. *Noblesse oblige.*"

What Guillermo Robledo said remains unresolved. If this is an issue resolved through the path of the "good Duhalde" it remains to be seen whether it was an exception, only to stop the burning tires and roadblocks, or if it means real change in the policies of job creation and reclaiming bankrupt companies.

Eduardo Duhalde arrived with Diego Kravetz. With a smile underneath his white beard, Duhalde said, "I'll take legal charge and the police will be withdrawn." More ovations and hugs. Duhalde, a man addicted to irony, comments to the lavaca writer, "Now I'm the clinic's trustee. When would you like an appointment?"

The police retreat, accompanied by more chants, and then comes the retaking of the clinic by the workers.

There were some surprises. The police had broken two doors and welded together the metal gate to prevent the hypothetical "worker invasion." They had broken some wooden chairs and the easel on which Plan A and Plan B were written, eaten the chicken that the workers were getting ready to have for lunch when they were forced out, and destroyed the MNER flags and signs. "This is what the judge wanted?" Elsa Montero asks.

"We're inside, the police are outside—we won," Hernán murmurs, concluding, "And if the government wants a fight, we'll give them a fight."

"We're going to do things within the law, or outside the law," Murúa says with the "good Duhalde" beside him, "but if the political will exists in this government that calls itself popular, then they should be discussing what kind of laws we need to change to restore an Argentina with jobs."

Traffic begins to move again. Some motorists honk their horns to show support. By now it's nighttime in Parque Centenario—the smell of burning tires has dissipated. The workers stay in the clinic, looking forward to having some kind of a good weekend.

Chapter Nine

Unión y Fuerza
A Two-Word Lesson

In 2001, after having been laid off by a model businessman, the Gyp Metal workers were standing under a bridge debating their future. Then they occupied the factory and managed to make it work. Today Unión y Fuerza (Union and Strength) is a leading company in its market. Its workers offer lessons on what management costs mean to a business.

The workers at Unión y Fuerza had a dilemma. "What do we do on May 1st—do we work or not? We met in assembly, discussed it, and the majority voted to come in to work to catch up on production." This is how Roberto Salcedo, who was previously the electrician at the Gyp Metal factory, tells it. He is now president of Unión y Fuerza, the cooperative that managed to occupy the factory, and after a six-month struggle, to expropriate it from its owners.

Unión y Fuerza specializes in manufacturing tubes of various alloys, in shapes and sizes including hollow and solid brass, and other semi-finished, non-iron metal products, used by innumerable industries.

It's one of the first reclaimed factories in a process that, in the last few years, has become a symbol of the contradictions and the possibilities that crisscross this puzzle called Argentina.

Today the cooperative has fifty-four members and employs another thirty workers (chosen among family and friends). They earn enough to make them feel uncomfortable revealing it in public, amid the Argentine economic malaise.

Salcedo winks and whispers, "We don't say how much we earn, so our wives don't find out."

All the workers earn the same. The cooperative is absolutely egalitarian. Another difference is its horizontality—the assembly makes the important decisions, which the Administrative Council then carries out.

The workers took charge of management (excuse the poor choice of words) by applying common sense—the mechanics and metalworkers may not have master's degrees, nor have they read the works of Peter Drucker. Nevertheless, they managed to salvage and make efficient and profitable a company that had gone bankrupt despite the lot of engineers, analysts, and accountants they once employed. Along the way they discovered that the factory's cancer was neither labor costs (according to the typical neoliberal rhetoric of the times) nor the country's crisis (typical owner's excuse), but managerial costs.

On August 18, 2000, the men who now sit in the director's office wearing overalls were standing under a bridge in Avellaneda, half a block from the factory, about to join this era's growing crowd of unemployed workers.

A decision was made.

"We decided to occupy the factory to demand the wages that they owed us and to defend our jobs," Salcedo explains. They had received suspension notices and the company was bankrupt. "We occupied the company. We tricked the doorman by telling him that we had forgotten some things inside. There were cops at the door, but once they opened the door and we set foot inside, we were in, and they never got us out again."

Shortly afterward, they discovered that the same doorman was one of the fronts who was supposedly one of the company's owners.

The Toilet Maneuver

What was the maneuver? It consisted of three very creative steps.

Gyp Metal belonged to Mr. "Beto" Wulfman. (His real name has long been forgotten.) Salcedo says, "It seems he wanted to make easy money by borrowing huge sums. They were four million dollars in debt. The company went to a creditors meeting and he requested the judge's authorization to sell the plant in order to avoid bankruptcy. The judge authorized it and he faked the sale of the plant to the doorman. The doorman was formerly homeless— he slept in a tiny 2 x 1.5 meter room that Wulfman even charged him rent to live in. If he hadn't signed as the front, Wulfman would have kicked him out."

Once the phony sale was done, the judge was told that the company was moving to another location. It was another farce. "In a rented garage they put two old machines and a toilet that didn't even have running water. They placed it directly on the floor to trick the trustee," Salcedo recalls. That way, when Wulfman was to file for bankruptcy, what would be auctioned were the old machines and the toilet, while he kept the original factory in the doorman's name.

The factory would later reopen with a new name, free of debt, out of bankruptcy, with the owner pocketing millions and looking to start the whole cycle all over again.

The fraud was attempted so shamelessly and with such impunity, that when the workers occupied the plant (supposedly sold and transferred to the garage with the dry toilet) they found that the directors had left all their personal belongings—glasses, calculators, agendas, etc.—knowing that they would continue working in those same offices a couple of days later. Salcedo explains, "They didn't fire the managers. They sacked us, leaving us without back wages, vacation pay, and bonuses they owed us. This way they also avoided paying taxes, suppliers, lawsuits, retirement funds, the telephone, electric, and gas bills—everything." Everything went into bankruptcy, to be paid off with the old machines and the toilet. The new company with a new name was to start with a blank slate.

But on that August 18th the workers decided to take matters into their own hands.

"We knew that it was a factory that could be profitable but had been managed by someone without scruples," Salcedo says. They began the resistance inside the factory. They collected donations from universities, they went to the courts, city governments, and ministries searching for a solution. Churches donated food.

The Idea

But resistance by itself is limited if it doesn't also have a plan to focus and maximize its potential. They wanted to reopen the factory, but a lawyer for the Metallurgical Workers' Union (UOM) told them that would be impossible. Salcedo remembers, "He told us that we had to go home and forget about being paid, because there was no way it was possible during a bankruptcy. He told us that we wouldn't be able to get the plant running again either, even if we tried, because if the owner, with his entire team of professionals and all his experience, ended up bankrupt, how could fifty workers with no experience manage to make it work? 'You have no capital, nothing,' they told us. It's not that they lacked the

The Movement

At the National Institute of Cooperatives and Social Economy (INAES), 970 cooperatives are registered. The first, the José Manuel Estrada Institute, dates back to 1953. Since then, their number has increased slowly, but steadily—until the turning point that the reclaimed factories movement represents. Between 2001 and September 2004, 290 cooperatives were organized in the city of Buenos Aires alone—representing 30 percent of the total. Artisans, cultural collectives, projects of popular assemblies and grassroots community media adopted the legal structure that most fit their principles—horizontal and autonomous. This also fulfilled their need to carve out economic and creative space to sustain themselves. These cooperatives recovered the scarcest commodity in Argentina: jobs. The minimum number of members needed to establish a cooperative is six, meaning that at least 1,740 jobs have been created in Buenos Aires since 2001.

will, because the UOM did help us. What they lacked was the idea that something could be done."

The other contact they had made during their visits to the Avellaneda town council was Councilwoman Liliana Caro. Her husband, Luis Caro, was a law student. Liliana proposed that he meet with them to see if there was an alternative to this death-foretold situation.

There was. The key idea was to support the factory's temporary expropriation by means of a provincial law in defense of public domain—then restart the bankrupt factory, create jobs, and produce. The law student came up with a solution that the politicians, government, functionaries, and unions had never imagined.

The Organization

The first problem was how to organize the cooperative. For a time, one member acted simultaneously as leader, treasurer, and jack-of-all-trades until it was clear that this distribution of power didn't work. "At the assembly the workers would say 'why did you do that?' or 'why didn't you consult us about that other thing?' It wasn't lack of trust in him personally, just that no one was convinced that one person could make all the decisions."

The problem was not the person, but the mechanism. They decided to change the Administrative Council, and, instead of the Council making decisions and then informing the assembly, the process was inverted—decisions began to be made collectively for the Council to carry out. Conflict resolved.

They were already aware of what their second problem would be—they had no capital to begin with. They thought that the factory could be profitable, and that assumption was confirmed, when right away, bank managers began showing up to offer them loans to restart production.

Against what any economic or financial guru would have advised, Unión y Fuerza rejected these offers.

Salcedo explains, "There are many companies that accept these loans, and, in the end, they end up belonging to the banks. Right?"

In addition, the factory's clients reappeared, offering to put up cash in exchange for a stake in the company. They also rejected these temptations. "If it looked like a good idea for these guys to put up cash and become partners, why not try to do things ourselves?"

They opted for maintaining their autonomy, invested part of the unemployment insurance they had received when they were fired, and bought a metalworking furnace with a kind of IOU to the city of Avellaneda to be paid in sixty days. They paid it back in thirty days, with real earnings from that first month of work.

With the customers, they accepted the following deal: the client would provide the raw materials and the cooperative would make the products and charge only for labor costs.

Salcedo sums it up saying, "That's how we recovered without accepting a single peso from anyone."

How did these men (none of whom have a university degree and most of whom do not even have a high school diploma) administer, manage, market, and run nothing less than an entire factory in the complex reality of today's market, economy, and finances?

"We wanted to go with a very small-time economy. Nothing complicated. Buy this, sell that, this much is left, and that's it. First we did an evaluation of the market."

And did any accountant or specialist help you with that?

"No, the guys did it—workers, machinists, mechanics. The first thing was to define the prices we would sell our products at. The idea was to find the old owner's electric, gas, and other bills. We knew how many tons were manufactured and what the expenses were. We divided everything by kilo, and that's how we knew how much each kilo of tubing produced cost us. We added up how much we were capable of producing and how much each of the co-operative members could make, and that's how we set the price, keeping the market price in mind. The math was very simple—the workers themselves did it. There were no engineers here…

Costs analysts?

"None of those things. We took the revenue, distributed if it was possible. But paying the gas, electricity, and those things came first, so we wouldn't have any debts."

The customers came back. One of the most unexpected of those was José Wulfman, the brother of the factory's previous owner. "I bought from my brother, but if he's no longer here, I have no problem buying from you guys," explained the man from the Wellman Company, located in the Haedo neighborhood. Like him, all the previous customers decided to continue with Unión y Fuerza.

The beginning was hard. As workers dependent on a boss, they earned 600 pesos a month. The cooperative began distributing no more than 200 pesos, "and sometimes not even that." But the mere accumulation of work began to change the outlook. "We would set aside part of the revenues for raw materials. That's how we built up our own stock and carried out the fabrication process entirely with our own resources."

The books worked out well. They discovered that one of the differences from the previous management was the managerial cost (despite the fact that even they had bought into the neoliberal mantra according to which modern economies don't work because of labor costs).

The company's owner—Salcedo says—would take home 25,000 pesos a month during hard times, and up to 50,000 if he thought it necessary. And there was a group of managers, "The engineer earned 6,000 pesos, and there were six or seven others at about that same figure, and another fifteen people making 3,500 to 4,000 pesos."

Meanwhile, Wulfman lived a carefree life. In the midst of the bankruptcy he was buying imported cars. He bought one of his sons a brand new foreign car, and a motorcycle for another son. "He had a hell of a chalet that I got to see one time when he had me go over to fix something. And get this—he didn't even intend to pay me for that job. He added a couple of hours to my paycheck—nickels and dimes."

He says this without resentment—chalking it up as one more aspect of a businessman character.

Now that you know both sides of the job, what differentiates the administration part from the production part?

"Workers drink *mate* without sugar—the office employees, coffee. That is always a difference and a sore spot. Now I discovered that you drink coffee in the office, not because you're more refined, but because you don't have the time or the space to drink *mate*. I would say that office work is less rewarding. You work with papers instead of torches and tools, but at the same time, you have other responsibilities, you don't have a set schedule, and you're vulnerable to making mistakes.

Salcedo's main advice for other factories facing the same situation is that there is no discussion if you're not inside the factory. "If you're inside, you can think about what kind of cooperative, what type of production. But if you're outside, you have no way to negotiate."

Another lesson learned is that you have to overcome fear. "You have to break through many fears, like the idea that you can't take over a company like this one. Actually, you learn how. And then you have the satisfaction that you are doing it for yourself."

He thinks that's why the workers' attitude is so different. "It's not the same when there is a supervisor looking over your shoulder, as when you are working for your own enterprise. There are compañeros here that come to work even when they're sick. If you're lazy, your own coworkers will come and tell you to get with it."

Salcedo explains that the factory currently produces between 60 and 70 tons of pipes, which makes it the leading supplier to the national market.

They have orders for exporting 150 tons to Mexico, but they can't fill the demand. "And we don't want to neglect the internal market, although I think that we can complement it with exports. We're looking into buying more machines, but we're going to do everything by taking our time about it and according to how the expropriation process is resolved."

That is when the workers will find out whether the capital they've accumulated will be used to pay for the final, court-approved expropriation or if they will be able to use those funds to continue growing. For now, they just know that it is in their interest to produce more. The plant runs 24 hours a day, with three shifts, and they've decided not even to shut down on May 1st (International Workers' Day). It was a decision made by the majority, in assembly, in a country full of unemployment, recession, and deindustrialization. They believe that in this way, they can continue to escape an economic model that had pushed them to the opposite of Unión y Fuerza—disunity and weakness.

Chapter Ten

Comercio y Justcia
The Future and the Glory

The prestigious Córdoba newspaper Comercio y Justicia *(Commerce and Justice) was reclaimed and purchased by its workers, organized in* La Prensa *(the Press) Cooperative. An unprecedented judicial decision avoided expropriation. The workers managed to edit a successful publication. Doing the opposite of what those who intended to keep the newspaper had in mind—they bet on journalism, quality, and an internal system of coexistence and decision-making that they consider revolutionary.*

It's common knowledge that in Argentina, glory is anything but eternal.

The newspaper *Comercio y Justicia* had been an influential publication on economic and judicial issues for sixty years, invoking the academic style of a province referred to as "*la docta.*"[1] It was never sold in newsstands, but only through subscriptions to professionals, businesses, and government agencies.

Like so many others, the newspaper was family property until the Eguías family sold it in the merger and acquisition frenzy that concentrated the media in fewer hands during the Menem and de la Rúa administrations. A Córdoban group—headed by the Eguías' lawyer, Vicente Aznar—purchased it in 1996. Aznar, in turn, resold it to the Brazilian group that edits Sao Paulo's *Gazeta Mercantil*, the fifth-most-read business newspaper in the world and owner of forty Brazilian newspapers. Each stage of this process made someone rich, although not exactly the workers, nor even the company itself.

For example: *Gazeta* paid Aznar $1 million for 40 percent of *Comercio y Justicia*. Once he took over the paper in April 2001, the Brazilian group's president, Luiz Fernando Ferreyra Lévy, traveled to Córdoba to promise the newspaper's one hundred workers that the company would have a "glorious future."

Ninety days later they already owed them a month and a half in wages.

They did, however, hire managers (at $8,000 a month) whom they housed at the Córdoba Sheraton. The rest of the managers raised their own salaries, including the editorial secretary's, by 1,000 pesos. Meanwhile they paid the workers in installments and didn't even make payments to their retirement plans or health insurance.

In August they stopped paying salaries. In September there was a strange robbery—which Córdoban Police Criminal Intelligence unofficially considered to be faked by the company—of forty-five computers, satellite decoders, digital memory servers, and electric generators, among other goods strategic to the newspaper. The stripping of the company's assets was under way.

The paradox: The workers brought their personal computers to keep the newspaper printing, but they also held strikes to demand payment of back wages.

With the invention of the so-called *corralito*,[2] the collapse was absolute. The series of assemblies and partial strikes ended in an all-out strike starting on December 11, 2001.

Diplomatic Balls[3]

The owners broke an administrative management record—they owed the workers five months of wages and their year-end bonuses in the midst of an economic collapse that is difficult to comprehend. When something in the economy makes no sense, the explanation tends to be found in a word that, at some point, had a clean connotation: laundering. "There have been many cases of companies going under in very similar situations, like what happened with all the Exxel Group companies," says Javier de Pascuale, the newspaper's director and member of the La Prensa Worker Cooperative.

One of the Brazilian executives—the lawyer Ailton Trevisan—admitted to the workers, "The newspaper's existence makes no sense." Seven months earlier they had promised them glory.

On December 18th there was a hearing at the Córdoban Labor Ministry. The Brazilian executives arrived as the building was literally catching on fire, in the midst of a conflict with municipal workers, with the *Comercio y Justicia* workers marching in the street with exploding firecrackers as background music. After sizing up the situation, Trevisan told the Labor Ministry functionaries that the newspaper's representatives would never come back to Argentina.

"In any normal country they would have ended up in jail just for saying that in front of the Labor Ministry. But here, nothing happened," says de Pascuale.

Slave Owners and Saying Hello

In the middle of these developments, the owners of a publication called *Info-Bae*, Argentines Daniel Hadad and Sergio Szpolski, appeared on the scene. Their product had no distribution in Córdoba, and they proposed to insert it into *Comercio y Justicia*, keeping on half of the workers at half their salaries. The offer was not attractive. De Pascuale says, "The word 'slave owner' should be applied not only to the Brazilians."

Javier tells how all this was happening while the media was undergoing a process of concentration that, in Córdoba, left Channel 12 and the city's main newspaper, *La Voz del Interior*, in hands of the Clarín Group, associated with *La Nación* in CIMECO.[4]

They had been told that the newspaper's existence made no sense. The workers decided that it made sense to form a cooperative. It was on April 9, 2002. They were still on the street.

Through pure stubbornness, the cooperative obtained legal permission to take over the newspaper's publishing, paying a monthly rent of 2,500 pesos. Faced with the vacuum left by the bosses, Judge Beatriz Mansilla de Mosquera didn't see this solution as generating more conflict.

In June the workers reentered the office. They found it dismantled. The scene: "The computer servers weren't there, parts of the rotary were missing, the telephone, electricity, and water were shut off.

The antenna from the Telam agency (Argentina's Associated Press) has a decoder—they had taken that as well. All this was to make it impossible for the newspaper to function," de Pascuale says.

They started bit by bit. "We had to go to Telecom (the telephone monopoly) to ask them to reconnect the phone. They didn't want to reconnect our line if we didn't pay the previous debt. We explained that the debt wasn't ours, that the line was for a cooperative. They told us no, that it was the same address. It was the same with everything."

In spite of everything, they managed to reinstall all utilities, in some cases paying for services in advance. How did they do it? At the shop, they found tons of old newspapers, leftover materials, and aluminum sheets used for printing. They sold the scrap and got the minimum cash to buy rolls of paper. "But we ran into a monopoly there as well, and had to resort to the black market." Translation: exorbitant markups. They had to buy the rolls at more than double their value. They barely bought enough paper for three or four editions.

In the newsroom, since they were not networked, each article was saved onto a floppy disk, carried to the editor, who worked on it and then took it, on the same disk, to the printer. Old-fashioned journalism. The entire photo archive had also been ransacked, so they downloaded photos from the Internet.

All this took place amid uncertainty about how the whole adventure would end, without a single private advertiser and with virtual silence from the media—they didn't publish a single article about *Comercio y Justicia*'s situation. "They barely congratulated the newspaper's relaunching once we hit the streets again."

The Relaunch

On June 20, 2002, the newspaper hit the streets after an absence of 200 days. In one month they got back 1,500 of the 3,600 subscribers. "We didn't go after the advertisers to buy the ad space for two pesos. We kept a high rate, and bet on our product. Since we succeeded in this way, the advertisers started coming in on their own."

After paying the bills, buying the paper, and paying the rent, the workers took home their first paychecks in August 2002—200 pesos each for the forty-three cooperative members. The amount later went up to 480 and then to 600. They also decided to save and to build up capital (at the sacrifice of reduced incomes) to be better covered in the future.

Everything can take a turn for the worse. For fifteen months the cooperative worked in peace, until they heard the news that Judge Mansilla de Mosquera had decided to open a call for bids to purchase the newspaper. This provoked the miraculous reappearance of Hadad and his people, the Clarín Group, and the Vila Group (whose chief lobbyist is the unforgettable Menem-era ex-minister José Luis Manzano, who has also acquired newspapers and television channels in Mendoza and Rosario in an expansive plan that often goes against economic logic).

Javier says, "They came running to take advantage of a publication which runs, thanks to its workers, at a low price. The only advantage we had was the opportunity to match the best offer. The base price was 1,120,000 pesos. If any of them offered 2 million, we could match that price and our offer would be given priority."

It so happens that cooperatives generally don't have access to the same amount of capital as the large corporate groups, so it seemed that this saga was destined to have a classic unhappy ending.

Is What's Legal Also Fair?

The Judge's stance toward the workers was one of open mistrust, according to de Pascuale. The first time she asked them how they planned to make the newspaper function, they answered that it would be through a cooperative. "She laughed," Javier recalls, "and said that the government, not the judicial system, should take care of social problems." She threw up every roadblock imaginable to each of the workers' actions. "It was hell," Javier assures.

When the idea of the open bidding came up, *Comercio y Justicia* was already working with the Superior Court, the Magistrate's Association, the bar association, and the provincial government itself. Two traditionally aggressive unions (the printers and the journalists) were also on the scene, and the cost of leaving the workers on the street was getting higher. This judge who said she didn't want to resolve social problems began to sense the risk of provoking them. There are indications that authorities in the judiciary and the provincial government pressed the judge to back off her tendency to create martyrs.

"Simultaneously, we began an arduous judicial process in which Dr. Luis Caro had a lot to do with overturning the judicial decision," de Pascuale explains. Caro is the president of the National Movement of Reclaimed Factories (MNFR). De Pascuale recalls the judge's barely suppressed relief and joy at discovering that Caro was giving the judicial argument to get past the impasse provoked by an auction that she herself had authorized.

Caro's testimony:

"We presented the judge an offer to directly purchase [the newspaper]. The Bankruptcy Law says that there has to be an auction. And we offered, as part of the payment, compensation for work already done, in other words, what the workers are owed. These are the things we justly request in the Bankruptcy Law reform."

"So how did you get the judge to change her mind?"

"We presented a document that talked about equity. We posed the idea that, if she strictly applied the law, that would be unjust, because it was the workers' efforts that revived the newspaper, and

Failed Attempts I

A record of some efforts that didn't pan out and the obstacles they faced:

• Cooperpac organized to take over a printing company that was shut down because a judge seized its machines to pay off its creditors.

• The members of La Láctea, in Diego de Alvear in Santa Fe province, couldn't start production of cheese and powdered milk because they couldn't get the most basic ingredient: the milk. Dairy farmers want to sell it to the big chains. For the same reason, La Germaniense didn't make it either. In 2004, the Italian multinational Parmalat bought it out.

• Cristalería de Cuyo (Cuyo Glassworks), a Mendoza-based plant, was bought by the Cattorini Brothers firm, located in Buenos Aires.

• Workers at the La Esperanza (Hope) engineering works in Jujuy are organized as a cooperative, but the courts haven't yet cleared them to take control, so they are working for the union.

they deserve the chance to carry it forward. The judge agreed with this interpretation and accepted the direct purchase by the cooperative at its fixed value. Many people had said it was impossible for her to change her mind, but she finally did. It was also the only possible option, because the Córdoban government didn't want to expropriate. The decision was huge, because it set a judicial precedent for other cases to be resolved this way.

Javier de Pascuale adds his journalistic analysis: "The decision comprehends that it's a trap and cheating the workers to lift a company out of bankruptcy, generate added value, and then in the end someone else keeps it because it is made available for the whole world to purchase, without the possibility of the cooperative competing with big business."

Obvious conclusion: The law is unjust. "Infinite injustice," Javier says.

"The judge used courtroom arguments saying that the judge is not a functionary who enforces the law, but a magistrate who applies justice. She recognizes that her duty is to be just and fair, and that, with those criteria, it made sense to suspend the auction and sell the company directly to the workers," de Pascuale says.

The newspaper was sold for 1,400,000 pesos. Part of it was paid with the credits, or debt, that the company held with the workers. "And we took 420,000 pesos in loans—a low-interest loan from the Banco Nación, another from the Foncap (Social Capital Fund),[5] and a third one in the form of personal loans taken by each member of the cooperative. We're paying them off in 20,000-peso monthly installments, which means we should be free by late 2005. But the newspaper is already ours."

Recovering Journalism

And what about the journalistic aspect? De Pascuale insists that they never forgot what the newspaper's natural audience was—all kinds of professionals, lawyers, accountants, business administrators, architects, doctors, and judicial personnel.

"We rescued a decades-old editorial viewpoint, in defense of the real economy, small and medium-sized businesses, and the alternatives that arise out of the crisis. Producers' solutions were to create associations, cooperatives, and all the imaginative proposals

Failed Attempts II

The regional food warehouse Santa Edena, in Entre Ríos province, was privatized under former president Menem and closed soon thereafter. Since then, workers have fought to open the plant and to have it expropriated. This has pitted them against Sergio Taselli, the same businessman who managed the Río Turbo mine where fourteen workers perished. The courts also want to award Taselli Concordia Jugos (Concordia Juice), another firm whose workers want to run on their own. As the workers tell it, the owner is counting on the explicit support of Santa Edena's leaders and other government officials.

La Mendozina was a processor of dried fruits and vegetables whose closure was only averted when its workers took over. To keep afloat, it merged with the San Martín, a producers group, and its CEO Mariano Acosta. In less than six months, workers' control was attained and San Martín had gained a new market.

that emerge with or without the government's support. This is reflected in the newspaper's business section."

Before the newspaper closed, during de la Rúa's administration, the copy editor was a Cavallist (adherent to the policies of de la Rúa's—and previously Menem's—Minister of Economy, Domingo Cavallo). And so was the main business columnist (who belonged to the Mediterranean Foundation)[6]. Now the columnist is a member of the group that came up with the Phoenix Plan, an idea for an alternative capitalism, to oppose neoliberalism, emphasizing national production, decreasing inequality, and redistribution of wealth.

There were also changes in the legal section. "We reflect the new schools of thought that refer to constitutional guarantees and the defense of civil rights. This doesn't have much of an audience in the Supreme Court, but it does in the lower courts. The world advances toward the protection of liberties, but here there are court rulings that stipulate even how to write an article or how to use conditional verbs." There are also sections and articles dedicated to the most advanced laws and standards referring to sexual, racial, and ethnic minorities.

Comercio y Justicia, in the cooperative's hands, works opposite to the way many media enterprises do. They seem to think that by lowering their price, striving to be mediocre, and cutting costs, they make more money. Javier says, "That's why the state of the Argentine media is deplorable. If you see the big picture, you'll see—first—the concentration of the media in a few hands in the 1990s. Then the easy money runs out and they start cutting costs—the editorial staff is cut and quality goes down. The media

were first consolidated, then cut back, and now it's pathetic."
Javier doesn't wish to be excessive or rude, but he recognizes that,
at times, the media circus makes him sick.

"We had to think backwards. If someone sets up a newspaper,
he hires four or five well-paid journalists and fifteen kids for pen-
nies, and that's it. But here we had to figure out how to give jobs
to the maximum number of people. We couldn't make it to a hundred people, for example. The ideal number was fifty. Could it be
fewer? Yes. Would it turn out well? No. Also, we wanted the work
to be in an environment that would revive the good side of journalism—really different from other newsrooms. A different style,
different relationships, a different humanity."

We should note that de Pascuale is not referring to a poetic or
philanthropic question here, but to the often forgotten issue of cooperation in the workplace. Different relationships. "The thing is,
we're all owners of the newspaper. The logic of the job changes, and
everyone does their best. There was a strong effort to improve the
quality of the product in recent months, and we're starting to see
the fruits of that labor, while other papers are closing or ceasing to
be perceived as important, prestigious, or credible publications."

The result, it is worth reiterating, is that, in the first month
(August 2003) there were 1,500 subscriptions. During 2004 they
surpassed 4,000, and the numbers continue to rise, despite *Comercio y Justicia* being one of the country's most expensive newspapers.

Inside the Cooperative

The cooperative decided not to pay equal salaries, instead paying differentiated wages according to responsibility (in the journal-

ist positions), and more hours worked (in the graphic/printing division). But nobody earns more than 30 percent above the base pay of 875 pesos. "Since things are going well, and we paid off our debt and are saving up, we've decided to distribute bonuses of 400 pesos each trimester," de Pascuale notes.

The managers are chosen annually, with rotation each year. Nobody can hold a management position for more than two years. Everyone really follows this policy—de Pascuale himself was the cooperative's president and has left the post in the hands of Eduardo Pogrobinki. The idea is for everybody to participate in the newspaper's management. The assemblies are biweekly, and the management council was expanded. Instead of three members, there are seven.

In the beginning they were forty-three members of the cooperative. Thirteen new members have since joined. As Javier tells it, "They are compañeros who have already worked with us, and we decided they should be part of the cooperative. Some [of the original cooperative members] were hesitant at first, saying, 'I held out through the worst part of the conflict, and now someone comes and has the same benefits as me.' We discussed it in assemblies, and we decided that it's all for the sake of growing. Everyone benefits, and it was well understood."

Comercio y Justicia prints Córdoba's second largest newspaper, *Hoy Día*, and re-edited some if its own additional publications, such as *Factor* (for economists, distributed with the newspaper on Mondays), *Semanario Jurídico* (a judicial weekly), *Nomenclador Cartográfico* (Córdoba's city guide) and *El Investor* (for the construction industry). The print shop has become the cooperative's second source of income, after the newspaper itself.

Eighty percent of their clients are unions, and human rights and activist organizations (such as HIJOS),[7] for whom they print magazines, pamphlets, and posters.

The Inner Revolution

Some argue that in reclaiming a factory by means of a cooperative, the workers replace the owners, but, in essence, things remain the same. The workers end up exploiting themselves under the logic of capitalism.

What does de Pascuale think? "There may be acquired habits, because of which you tend to assume yourself dependent on someone. Or, in a management position, you reproduce the bosses' model. Cooperative education should change that. But I think that there's a huge difference between work and exploitation that has to do with where the fruits of the work end up. It has to do with there not being a difference between the useful value of your work and the exchange value of the results of your work. The cooperative system is totally fair because the results go to the people that produce them. Unless you think that working a lot is self-exploitation. I don't think that's true. Inside, we have a setup that goes against the logic of capitalism. A humanized work regime, a production arrangement decided by the workers themselves. In relationships outside the institution, we can't detach ourselves from the economy's logic, but we give ourselves the luxury of doing work for free and doing what we decide as workers. On the inside the revolution has already happened. And looking externally, our biggest contribution is demonstrating that workers can efficiently run an enterprise."

According to the facts available, the Brazilian media moguls were wrong.

The newspaper's existence makes sense.

Perhaps it is worthwhile to remember something else that has been reclaimed—a couple of words that seemed to have been kidnapped years ago: work and justice, to name just some of the words that continue to tell this story.

Chapter Eleven

The Movements

Sharing Knowledge and Combining Forces

Two large movements group together most reclaimed factories and companies. They play a key role in their legal defense, as well as in acts of resistance.

Almost by accident, the workers of the first reclaimed factories found themselves rescuing the machines abandoned by their bosses. They knew they could operate them, but they doubted whether they should.

The Federation of Worker Cooperatives was the first organization that gave them a hand and encouraged them to take a giant step. Nonetheless, this entity had been designed for small businesses and did not have the resources required by these new challenges posed at the turn of the century in Argentina. Tied to the old laws of cooperativism, the organization could not represent all the workers who dared to challenge the principle of private property.

The bankrupt factories began to reopen far outside the lime-
light, but their experiences traveled by word of mouth at a speed
that only the workers involved noticed. As the cases accumulated,
workers from different factories found common problems and
common enemies. They also found pragmatic and ingenious solutions along the way. Many self-managed enterprises, therefore,
considered it necessary to come together to share knowledge and
combine forces for the struggle. The first (short-lived) attempt was
the National Federation of Worker Cooperatives at Reconverted
Companies (FENCOOTER). Then the National Movement of
Reclaimed Companies (MNER) and the National Movement of
Worker-Reclaimed Factories (MNFR) were born, both presided
over by activists with Peronist backgrounds. Both are organizations oriented toward strategically defending the cooperatives
legally, as well as mobilizing to resist attempts to evict workers.
They also work toward coordinating communication among the
cooperatives about their different experiences.

A significant number of cooperatives also decided to go their
own way, without involving themselves in either of these organizations. And for a couple of years there was also a third group—the
National Summit of Reclaimed Factories en Lucha, that brought
together those companies that were linked to leftist parties who rejected the cooperative model and vied for nationalization under
workers' control. This group dissolved after some time, especially
after the Brukman workers decided to form a cooperative.

Beyond all the divisions, perhaps the biggest legal achieve-
ment for the reclaimed companies was a shared victory. On November 25, 2004, the Buenos Aires city legislature approved a de-

finitive Expropriations Law for thirteen cooperatives, whose workers must pay for the property at its bankruptcy value, over twenty years in biannual installments, after a three-year grace period. MNER and MNFR members, who were sitting opposite each other in the audience at the session when the law passed, looked at it other and chanted, "Workers united! And if you don't like it, screw you!"[1]

"Occupy, Resist, Produce"
Interview with Eduardo Murúa

President of the National Movement of Reclaimed Companies (MNER)

When was the National Movement of Reclaimed Companies created?

As a movement, it was born in the year 2000, when some companies that had been reclaimed began to get together with sectors that came from the social economy[2] movement. At first we formed what was called the Movement for a Social Economy, that brought together some factories—IMPA and Yaguané—some collective organizations, like the Quilmes Housing Cooperative and an electric cooperative from Moreno, and the Federation of Worker Cooperatives of Buenos Aires Province (FECOOTRA). Then some other companies approached us, like the ones José Avelli had met with in Rosario. Then we organized a plenary session at the IMPA plant and decided to launch the Movement. The FECOOTRA people decided not to join because we proposed that the mission be broader, that it stand for what we represent as workers, not just as cooperative members.

What was the difference?

We thought the Movement had to take on not just the reclaiming of companies, but also the union struggles and the political discussions within the working class. The new methods of protest that we had used in isolated cases could be multiplied. It made no sense to form part of a federation that would only fight to consolidate co-operatives. We proposed not only consolidating our own factory, but also to stand in solidarity with other workers in the same situation as us, and to share our experience with the world. This is what defined the Movement. The Federation of Worker Cooperatives, on the other hand, comes from a different background—it was formed by entrepreneurs, not by reclaimed enterprises.

What are MNER's guiding principles?

From the beginning we came out to propose to struggling workers that not one more job could be lost in Argentina. And we came up with the slogan: Occupy, Resist and Produce. We knew that the only possible road for reclaiming factories lay outside the legal framework, because we didn't have a law that defended jobs.

Do you mean that there is no law, or the law doesn't defend everyone equally?

For workers in Argentina there is no law. It only exists for the powerful. Since the restoration of democracy [after the 1976–1983 military dictatorship], all the laws that have been passed are against workers' rights. The laws, enacted first by the dictatorship and then by the formal democracy, served to consolidate a global economic model organized according to the international division of labor. The changes to the bankruptcy law, for example, had left us without the possibility of severance pay. The reformed law also requires the judge to liquidate a bankrupt company's assets in 120 days. The only way to reclaim the company is to occupy it and show, first the judge, and then the political class, that we're not going to leave the factory. If we were stuck outside, asking the judge to keep it open, we would get nowhere. If we were to ask politicians, we'd get even less. Only through occupation could we recover the jobs. After "occupy," we say you have to resist, because it takes time to convince the judicial and political sectors. Meanwhile, you have to avoid getting kicked out. And, lastly, to produce is to consolidate the process.

To occupy a factory as a way of opposing a legal system…. Were people afraid of this?

Certainly, if there weren't so many doubts and fears among the entire working class, there would be many more reclaimed factories. Because of these uncertainties, this process only works in places where there is some level of organization and capable leadership. The last company we reclaimed here was Ceres (a textile plant). On Friday we had agreed to occupy the factory on the following Monday, but as I was on my way there, the workers called me on my cellphone and told me that they didn't want to go in. I got there and kicked the door in. That's how they went in. Some workers are not organized and it's hard for them to rebel against the legal framework. It's hard for people to believe that the country's entire judicial and legal structure is always against them. They trust the system, and we sometimes lose conflicts for that reason.

In a country where private property is sacred, how do you manage to twist political arms to expropriate a factory?

In most cases, what has been expropriated was a bankrupt company—a property in the hands of a judge who was supposed to liquidate it. In these cases you don't affect many interests. But it's true that we question not only private property but the system itself.

Do you define yourselves as anticapitalist?

I, for one, do. And the Movement as well, because it wants the abolition of an oppressive system that generates joblessness and poverty, death, that can't even sustain the working class. But in the case of most reclaimed enterprises we're not affecting the interests of private property—we had no opposition from the banks, since when a company is liquidated, they hardly recover anything. And the suppliers that had credit with the company begin to work with us. I think that what the political class hasn't understood is the necessity of having this kind of enterprise. If there were a governmental policy for this sector we would have 200,000 workers at reclaimed companies. In a country where 90 percent of GNP is generated by 500 multinationals, it's very difficult for us to threaten the existence of private property.

Nonetheless, if you read the editorials in La Nación, *for example, it seems that we're facing a revolution...*

We face firm opposition from some dinosaurs, but what bothers us the most is the schizophrenic rhetoric coming from progressives. For example, we opened some factories together with Aníbal Ibarra (mayor of Buenos Aires), or President Kirchner will meet with us, but neither of them has a clear policy for regenerating employment. Don't even get me started about Felipe Solá (governor of the province of Buenos Aires). In his case, when everything blew up, the expropriations fell in line right away. Today, to obtain an expropriation, we have to mobilize every day, pressure, go all over the place, to argue the same thing every day.

What's the reason for this schizophrenia?

It's because they're still working within the framework of the reconstruction of capitalism. They think that the market will solve everything and that the state should simply be a mediator and provider of social support. In the city there has been a policy regarding the reclaimed factories for six years, but there is no acting organism to accompany the workers in order to make the process more viable. There's not even a way to make economic deals that are more favorable to the whole of the population. Expropriation is expensive. If there was a clear governmental policy and they accompanied the workers in the bankruptcy negotiations with the judge and trustee, we would surely get the companies at better prices. The debts owed to the government and the workers could be compensated and we could keep the factories without expropriation or the taxpayers spending anything.

What relationship does the Movement aim to have with the government?

Reclaiming companies should be a government policy, and the government should play a more active role. But, at the same time, it would be a strategic mistake to allow the government to manage companies that have been reclaimed and democratized by their workers. Imposing a government administration would mean that the workers are solely manual laborers who don't understand the company's management or its relationship to the economy as a whole. In a reclaimed company, one begins to deal with everything, while when you're a government employee, all you do is go to work and get paid, and not participate in the company's management.

Why is it that the companies that go bankrupt under owner management become profitable once the workers take them over?

For two reasons. Most of these companies were profitable and went bust because of financial problems, because of the debts they had accumulated. If they weren't in debt, they would have profits. If you take over the company without the owner's debt, that's already an important step. Another issue is that you no longer have to consider the profit margin that the owner would take, nor the managerial costs that the company had. That allows for recovery, independent of the technical conditions.

What role did the unions play in reclaiming factories?

The only one that had an important and serious role was the Quilmes UOM (Metallurgical Workers' Union), who formally supported the establishment of the cooperatives. Most unions didn't adopt this as a policy. Now the Graphic Federation is supporting this process in some cases, like the Patricios Cooperative. The Pharmaceutical Union, in the case of the Franco Inglesa Pharmacy, is also supportive. But, generally, the big unions never fight for the workers. This is how it worked: when a company went

bankrupt, they figured out how much the workers' severance payment should be and then told them to go sing to Gardel.[3]

How is the Movement organized internally?

The Assembly, composed of one worker from each company, is the
highest decision-making body. We don't establish representation
according to the number of workers in each company. Each company has one vote. We do it this way because we believe that one
of the labor movement's mistakes is that the bigger companies
have more weight in the unions, which leads to avoiding strikes by
negotiating with the big corporations, disregarding what the needs
of the workers as a whole may be. If we put together an organization in which the representatives of the bigger companies have
more weight, the day may come when these big firms negotiate an
agreement with the government and leave the smaller companies
out. We decided: one vote per worker in the company, and one
vote per company in the Movement. We also have representatives,
those of us who have stepped up the most and begun to talk, and
that's the way it is.

Are these representatives retractable, do they have term limits?

The organization is pretty anarchistic. We haven't even discussed
it. What we do try to do is to represent what the whole of the
workers think. We hold assemblies every month, month and a
half, because geographically we are scattered throughout the Re-
public, and we also lack resources. This is a social organization,
not a political organization, traditionally speaking. There's no reason to have everything defined, just the principal aims.

What are they?

An expropriations law, a 10,000-peso subsidy for each recovered job, bank loans to the worker cooperatives, and a specific retirement plan. The other thing we prioritize is the necessity of solidarity with the workers.

How does this solidarity take shape on a daily basis?

Participating in the conflicts that arise, standing with our compañeros, and when they are facing eviction, mobilizing all the factories together. Also, sometimes a factory will lend another some money—just a little—to buy the initial materials to get started. But there isn't a lending system. The relationship we have with the government sometimes allows us to provide some basic groceries to the struggling workers, or to a worker who has lost his job. Sometimes we can even get a *plan social* (essentially, unemployment benefits).

How are the factories organized internally?

In most cases they are democratic, with assemblies every year and elected councilors. Many workers have participated in the Council. At IMPA over these six years about sixty different workers have served on the Administrative Council. But it's the assemblies that really lead the factories—that define the general administration. The Administrative Council takes care of the day-to-day activity. We have problems in some factories because some workers imitate the owners' mechanisms, their hierarchies. We had to remind some of them that this is a reclaimed enterprise. There has to be an assembly, nobody is the owner who can decide by himself. Even if his ideas are right, everything has to be resolved in assembly. There were also some problems for female workers because some were being paid less for the same job.

Why do you think these things happen?

Because we continue to copy the culture we were taught. That's why for us, it's important to have egalitarian income. Nonetheless, there are workers who want to implement income scales like they had before. There are companies that recover as soon as a month after their bankruptcy, and others go through a tougher process and struggle. It takes more sacrifice to reclaim them, but when they achieve it, the workers there are more united and have really strong morals. In the ones where they go back to work sooner, the concept of solidarity isn't internalized as much. There wasn't a change, a struggle that deepened that idea of solidarity. Each worker does his part and thinks he should earn as much as before, according to his position.

Can egalitarian salaries be sustained in practice?

At IMPA we've all been earning the same for six years. We strive to place the moral incentives above the material ones. It's true that sometimes it seems unfair, because the best, most productive teams—the ones who collaborate the most, who struggle the most, who practice the most serious solidarity and take to the streets— earn the same as others who do their job well, but take off at 3 p.m. Sometimes the compañeros who participate the most say, "Hey, are we wrong? Shouldn't we make more since we're the ones that operate the machines, but who are also the ones here when there's a problem?" The egalitarian distribution of income is what locks in the element of unity.

Does the Movement have a position regarding the management team of reclaimed enterprises?

We consider it unnecessary.

But there are companies that do have one....

No, there aren't. The only experience is Zanello—which is structured as a corporation. The workers there weren't able to do anything other than form a workers' cooperative to achieve active participation within the corporation. Yes, sometimes management specialists are hired for marketing, but not in most cases.

Are those salaries different from the workers'?

There are differentiated wages if the compañero is contracted and isn't part of the cooperative.

And what happens when a cooperative realizes that it needs to expand its workforce?

We always request that workers that are brought in join the cooperative as members after a trial period. We don't want workers to be just employees because that ends up reproducing the dependency model that we're fighting against. We had problems in factories where the cooperative workers considered that it was better to hire workers than to make them members of the cooperative. If you're not prepared to allow people to join the cooperative because there might not be enough work for everyone later on, it's preferable not to take on the risk of having to fire people later for lack of work.

Is there a risk of turning into a boss?

That is a risk. That's the fear I personally have in this Movement—that some companies may degenerate and the workers in them become new bosses.

Is there any way to avoid this problem?

The workers' assemblies and maintaining the permanent state of discussion and understanding. The thing is, we haven't been around very long. For now, we have an adult education program that some workers from our companies are participating in. There's a course in forming a cooperative there. But I think it's not enough. There has to be training every day. We should have leadership teams at all the factories. Sometimes we don't have them.

Does the creation of cultural centers at the factories have anything to do with this need?

Through the cultural centers we are giving back to the people what they gave us when they supported us. We exist thanks to their support, not just because they sometimes mobilize in support of the companies, but also because the general public agrees with us. These spaces need to be used by the people—for culture, jobs, education, health . . . whatever they may be needed for. This also works toward consolidating our project. At most enterprises we still don't have definitive ownership of the property. At any moment we could find ourselves under a government that wants us out, or a judge that wants to evict us—then we'll need the peoples' support. It's like an umbrella for each company. At IMPA we did it for both reasons.

How does your organization differ from the National Movement of Reclaimed Factories?

At first we were all together, though it's been a long time since then. They didn't agree with us taking political stances, or acting in solidarity with other groups struggling for their causes. Furthermore, we were unable to maintain a relationship after Luis Caro, president of the Movement of Factories, ran for mayor of Avellaneda on the ballot with Aldo Rico,[4] who was running for governor.

The MNER has an elected representative. Why did the Movement strive to place one of its own in the Buenos Aires Legislature?

The Movement is independent of the state and the political parties, but is has a legislator because we consider it important to have institutional access to the government. We've always believed that the social movements have to sit at the political table. When we saw that Miguel Bonasso[5]—who comes from Montoneros,[6] like I do—had the possibility of winning a seat, I approached him to see if we could form an alliance. At first the discussion was very profound and we thought about creating a national movement—but it didn't work because of our differences regarding Kirchner's government. Instead of being a new actor, it ended up being an electoral alliance for each to get what he wanted.

Would you repeat the experience?

Yes. But we would have to run on our own, or with a social organization, to propose a different solution for the people. The struc-

ture of the party bureaucracy apparatus is very large. And we have
neither the media, nor the money, nor the outreach to battle it
out. We have solidarity teams and the social movement leaders,
but it's very hard to go against the government's—the state's—apparatus, against the parties and the public figures they plant in the
media during an election. It takes a tremendous effort to participate in an election—there aren't very many of us, and we try to
prioritize our organization or center our efforts on the recovery of
jobs. As of now there is nothing decided. It will be a tactical question—perhaps we'll make the decision two or three months before
the election, like we did with Bonasso.

Resources

Programs

El Programa Trabajo Autogestionado (self-managed work program), sponsored by the Employment Secretary of the Work, Employment, and Social Security Ministry, offers economic assistance of up to 150 pesos a month to workers in self-managed enterprises or to those in the process of recovering their workplace. In addition, it offers a grant to workplaces of 500 pesos per worker, up to 50,000 total pesos.

Address: Avenida Leandro N. Alem 650
Phone: 4310 5 706-1012
Email: trabajoautogestionado@trabajo.gov.ar

The General Sarmiento National University supports a multidisciplinary team of technical advisors to help recovered companies make evaluations, diagnose problems, and devise solutions. One of their goals is to facilitate coordination, create networks, and encourage trade between recovered enterprises.

Phone: 4469 7731

Email: Daniel Cassano: dcassano@ungs.edu.ar; Raquel Arévalo: rarevalo@ungs.edu.ar; Mabel Rios: mrios@ungs.edu.ar; Silvia Sanchez: ssanchez@ungs.edu.ar

On the Web

Argentine Federation of Workplace Cooperatives

www.fecootra.org.ar

Web site of the Argentinian Federation of Workplace Cooperatives that includes information on recovered factories and workplaces.

Foro Cooperativo

www.eListas.net/lista/cooperativo

Email discussion list created to promote cooperatives and communication between them.

National Movement of Reclaimed Factories (MNFR)

www.fabricasrecuperadas.org.ar

Official Web page of the MNFR. This Web site grew out of a training workshop cosponsored by lavaca.org and the organization Hipatia, an advocate of freeware and open source software.

National Movement of Recovered Companies (MNER)

www.mnerweb.com.ar

Web site of MNER, designed by an MNER-member recovered company specializing in Web design.

The Take

www.thetake.org

The Web site based on Avi Lewis and Naomi Klein's documentary *The Take*, with a lot of information on the movement of recovered workplaces in Argentina and worldwide. Mostly in English.

Z Magazine and ZNet

www.zmag.org; www.znet.org

Z Magazine and its affiliated Web site ZNet carry many reports about the movement in Argentina, both in English and Spanish.

Books and pamphlets

Capón Filas, Rodolfo, ed. 2003. *Cooperativas de trabajo* (La Plata: Plantense). More than twenty articles by professionals from different disciplines, mostly focusing on legal aspects of recovered workplaces.

Fajn, Gabriel, ed. *Fábricas y empresas recuperadas: Protesta social, autogestión y ruptura en la subjetividad.* (Buenos Aires: Ediciones del Instituto Movilizador de Fondos Cooperativos) Report from a group of researchers from the Centro Cultural de la Cooperación (Cooperative Cultural Center).

Ghioldi, Carlos. 2004. *Supermercado Tigre: Crónica de un conflicto en curso* (Rosario: Prohistoria). An eyewitness account by union activist Ghioldi about the struggle to take over this Rosario-based supermarket.

Heller, Pablo. 2004. *Fábricas ocupadas: Argentina, 2000–2004*

(Buenos Aires: Ediciones Rumbos). A worker's account of the struggle at Sasetru and Transportes del Oeste, among others, written from the perspective of a member of the socialist Partido Obrero.

Magnani, Esteban. 2003. *El cambio silencioso: empresas y fábricas recuperadas por los trabajadores en la Argentina* (Buenos Aires: Prometeo). Journalistic account by one of the producers of Lewis and Klein's *The Take*.

Secretaria de Desarrollo Económico del Gobierno de la Ciudad Buenos Aires. *Empresas recuperadas.* Study written by an arm of the Buenos Aires city government, also available online at http://www.buenosaires.gov.ar/areas/produccion/subs_produccion/apoyo_empresas_recuperadas.php.

Carpinero, Enrique, and Mario Hernández, eds. 2002. *Produciendo realidad: Las empresas comunitarias* (Buenos Aires: Topia). This is one of the first books written about the movement of recovered workplaces. It includes accounts of the early days at Zanón, Brukman, and Grissinópoli.

Guide to Factories and
Recovered Companies

Industry	Factory/Company	City/Province
Food		
Beverages	15 de Noviembre	Pablo Nogués (PBA*)
Meat	Avícola Moreno/ formerly San Sebastián	Moreno (PBA)
	Former employees of Minguillón meat processors	Moreno (PBA)
	Frigocarne Máximo Paz	Máximo Paz (Santa Fe), Cañuelas (PBA)
	J. J. Goméz	General Roca (Río Negro)
	Puerto Vilelas	Puerto Vilelas (Chaco)
	San Justo	San Francisco (Córdoba)
	Santa Isabel	Santa Isabel (Santa Fe)
	Yaguané	La Matanza (PBA)
Candy	Alimentaria San Pedro	San Pedro (PBA)
Fruit	Cachepunco	Santa Clara (Jujuy)
	Union saladeña/formerly Pindapoy	Saladas (Corrientes)
Grain	Molinera de Saladillo	Saladillo (PBA)
Frozen confections	Vieytes/Ghelco	Capital Federal

* Province of Buenos Aires

Dairy products	Ameghino	Ameghino (PBA)
	Blaquier	Florentino Armeghino (PBA)
	Llampicó	Ayacucho (PBA)
	Montecastro	Capital Federal
Baking	Alimentcia Lanús	Remedios de Escalada (PBA)
	El Aguante	Vicente López (PBA)
	La Argentina	Capital Federal
	La Nueva Esperanza/Grissinópoli	Capital Federal
Pasta and empanadas	Mil Hojas	Rosario (Santa Fe)
	Resurgir	Rosario (Santa Fe)
	Sasetru	Avellaneda (PBA)
Snacks	Malvinas Argentinas	Malvinas Argentinas (PBA)
Supermarkets	Former employees of San Cayetano Pergamino	Buenos Aires and environs
	Trabajadores en Lucha (Workers in Struggle)/ formerly Supermercado Tigre	Rosario (Santa Fe)
Auto parts	19 de Diciembre	Villa Ballester (PBA)
	Cristal San Justo	La Matanza (PBA)
	Felipe Vallese	Quilmes (PBA)
	Forja San Martín	San Martín (PBA)
	Galaxia	Ruta 2 (PBA)
	Mecber	Berazategui (PBA)
	Ruedas Rosario/formerly Cimetal	Rosario (Santa Fe)
	San Carlos	Sarandi (PBA)
	Vélez Sarfield	Quilmes (PBA)
Shoes and sportswear	Chamical/ex Gatic	Chamical (La Rioja)
	Union de Trabajadores Sanluiseños/ formerly Gatic	San Luis del Palmar (Corrientes)
	Unidos por el Calzado/formerly Gatic	San Martín (PBA)

Construction

Quarries	Nueva Salvia	Puerto de Buenos Aires; Entre Ríos

	Olavarría	Olavarría (PBA)
	Cantera Sime	Victoria (Entre Ríos)
Ceramics	Argypaz	José C. Paz (PBA)
	Cerámica Cuyo	Guaymallén (Mendoza)
	Cerámicos Marabó	General Rodriguez (PBA)
	Coceramic	Paraná (Entre Ríos)
	Palmar	Laferrere (PBA)
	FaSinPat/Zanón	Parque Industrial (Neuquén)

Cosmetics

Roby   Ruta 3 (PBA)

Leather

Obreros Unidos del Cuero   Lanús (PBA)

Education

Educo	Capital Federal
Fishbach	Capital Federal
Insituto Comunicaciones	Capital Federal
Jardín de Palermo	Charcas
Tomás Espora	Adrogué (PBA)

Electrical products

Electrounión   San Andrés (PBA)

Restaurants

| Quilla Hue | General Roca (Río Negro) |
| Nubacoop | Terminal de Ómnibus de Rosario (Santa Fe) |

Graphic arts/printing

| Cefomar | Capital Federal |
| Campichuelo | Capital Federal |

Compagraf/formerly Gatic	San Martín (PBA)
Chilavert	Capital Federal
Graficos Asociados	Mendoza Capital
Grafi-co	San Martín (PBA)
Gráfica del Sol	Capital Federal
Gráfica Mercatalli	Capital Federal
Gráfica Patricios/formerly Conforti	Capital Federal

Gasoline, heating, and cooking gas

Cooperagas las Armas	Maipú (PBA)
Cootragas San Miguel	San Miguel (PBA)
Ecoopgas Arrecifes	Ruta Provincial 51 (PBA)
Punta Arenas	Capital Federal
Obreros VDB	Avellaneda (PBA)
Sigas	La Matanza (PBA)

Hotels

BAUEN (Buenos Aires Una Empresa Nacional)	Capital Federal
Cacique Pismanta	Distrito las Flores (San Juan)
Marsur	Mar Chiquita (PBA)

Computer services/Web design

Newen	Capital Federal

Wool processing

Lavalán	Avellaneda (PBA)

Lumber

La Fábrica	Ayacucho (PBA)
Maderera Córdoba	Capital Federal
Maderera Santiago	Rawson (San Juan)
Sur Coop	Concordia (Entre Ríos)

Automobile mechanics

Talleres Universal	Bernal (PBA)

Tools and implements

Herramientas Union	Rosario (Santa Fe)
Metalmecánica	General Pico (La Pampa)

Manufacturing

Tractors and trailers	Cañadense	San Martín (PBA)
Weapons	Reno	Lanús (PBA)
Heating and air conditioning	11 de Noviembre	San Antonio de Areco (PBA)
	Evaquil	Quilmes Oeste (PBA)
	Fader	Rosario (Santa Fe)
	IMPOPAR (Industria Metalúrgica Popular Argentina/formerly Inpopar)	Parque Industrial Tandil (PBA)
	MVH	Villa Martelli (PBA)
Household appliances	2 de Diciembre/Coventry	José Leon Suarez (PBA)
	CIAM (Cooperativa Industrial Argentina Metalúrgica Julián Moreno)/SIAM	Avellaneda (PBA)
	Renacer/formerly Aurora	Ushuaia (Tierra del Fuego)
Storage	Adabor	Florencio Varela (PBA)
	IMPA (Industria Metalúrgica y Plástica Argentina)	Capital Federal
Shelving	Crometal	Berazategui (PBA)
Hardware	Argentina Nueva Era	Villa Martelli (PBA)
	La Histórica	General Pico (La Pampa)
	La Matanza	Isidro Casanova (PBA)
	La Unión	Sarandi (PBA)
Metal fabrication	25 de Mayo	Quilmes (PBA)
	Fundición LB	Laferrere (PBA)
	Metal Varela	Florencio Varela (PBA)
Machines and parts	Metalúrgica Lanús	Lanús (PBA)

Motors	Metalúrgica las Varillas/Zanello	Las Varillas (Córdoba)
	Campos	San Martín (PBA)
	Diógenes Taborda	Capital Federal
Motors	Electromecánica Barrancas	Rosario (Santa Fe)
	Villa Elisa	La Plata (PBA)
Piping and tubing	Los Constituyentes	Villa Martelli (PBA)
	Unión y Fuerza	Sarandi (PBA)
Stainless steel	Copacinox	Lanús (PBA)
Stone	La Dorrego	Quilmes Oeste (PBA)
Furniture	Muebleş San José	San Andrés (PBA)
Boats	Navales Unidos	Dock Sud (PBA)

Paper products

Packing materials	Bolsas Olavarría	Parque Industrial Olivarría 1 (PBA)
	Cooperpel	Capital Federal
Paper	Papelera 8 de Marzo	Urquiza 718 Adolfo Alsina (PBA)
	Unión Papelera Platense	La Plata (PBA)

Communications/journalism

	Comunicar	Villa María (Córdoba)
	La Prensa	Mariano Moreno 378 (Córdoba)
	LU3 Radio del Sur	Bahía Blanca (PBA)

Paint

	Cintoplom	Ciudadela Sur (PBA)

Plastics

	Viniplast	Capital Federal
	Vinil-plast	Quilmes (PBA)

Chemicals   Química del Sur   Berazategui (PBA)

Health

Clinics	22 de Junio	Mercedes (PBA)
	Ados	Avenida Argentina 1000 (Neuquén)
	Fénix Salud/formerly IMECC	Capital Federal
	Clínica Junín	Dean Funes 581 (PBA)
	Las Flores Salud	Las Flores (PBA)
	Unión y Trabajo	San Martín 151 y 343 (La Rioja)
Pharmacies	Franco Inglesa	Capital Federal
Hospitals	Hospital Israelita	Terrada 1164/Nazca 1164
	Hospital de Llavallol	Llavallol (PBA)

Bathroom fixtures

	Fénix	Lanús Oeste (PBA)
	Porcelana Sanitaria Malvinas Argentinas	Ruta Panamericana (PBA)

Building services

	Porteros	Capital Federal

Textiles

Clothing	18 de Diciembre/Brukman	Capital Federal
	Ceres	Capital Federal
	Confecciones Gaiman	Gaiman (Chubut)
	Entre-Confec/formerly Angelo Paolo	Ciudad de la Paz (Entre Ríos)
	Textil San Remo (former)	Lanús Oeste (PBA)
	Textil Pampeana	Santa Rosa (La Pampa)
Industrial	Inimbo	Resistencia (Chaco)
Fabric	Textiles Pigüé/formerly Gatic	Pigüé (PBA)

Transport

3 de Julio	Zárate (PBA)
Confortable	Avenida Vélez Sarfield (Córdoba)
El Petróleo	Cutral-Co (Neuquén)
La Nueva Mitre	Nationwide
Posadas	Valdepeña (Corrientes)
Transporte del Oeste	Merlo (PBA)
Yacanto	Córdoba (Córdoba)

Glass

Industrial Glassware		
	Cooptem	Villa Dominico (PBA)
	11 de Junio	Berazategui (PBA)
	Crista Avellaneda	Avellaneda (PBA)
	Maná	Villa Dominico (PBA)
	Vitrofin	Canada de Gómez (Santa Fe)

More information is available on each of these companies on lavaca.org's Web site site at http://lavaca.org/seccion/actualidad/0/308.shtml.

Notes

Introduction: Workers of Another Class

1. Smith, Adam, *The Wealth of Nations* (London: Methuen and Co., Ltd. 1776).

2. Bell, Daniel, *The Coming of Post-industrial Society* (New York: Basic Books, 1973).

3. Bauman, Zygmunt, *Society Under Siege* (Cambridge: Polity Press, 2002).

4. Ibid.

5. Harvey, David, *The New Imperialism* (New York: Oxford University Press, 2003).

6. Zibechi, Raúl, *El nuevo imperialismo y America Latina* (*The New Imperialism and Latin America*), April 29, 2004, alainet.org.

7. *Trabajo basura*, or "trash job," is a term used in Argentina to describe part-time, low-wage, under-the-table pay, no-benefits jobs in the service sector, such as at fast-food restaurants and grocery stores. A similar term in the United States is "McJobs."

8. Bourdieu, Pierre, *La misère du monde* (*The Misery of the World*) (Paris: Editions du Seuil, 1993). The English-language quotations here are from a Spanish translation of Bourdieu.

9. Quoted in Bell, *Coming of Post-industrial Society*, 29.

10. Dahrendorf, Ralf, *Class and Class Conflict in an Industrial Society* (Stanford, CA: Stanford University Press, 1959).

11. Bell, *Coming of Post-industrial Society*, 37.

12. Zibechi, Raul, *La imposible reconstrucción del estado benefactor* (*The Impossible Reconstruction of the Welfare State*), www.lavaca.org.

13. "Miseria planificada" ("Planned Misery") is the title of an article written by Sergio

Ciancaglini and published by the newspaper *El País* of Spain and the *International Herald Tribune*. It was republished in the book *Argentina, país desperdiciado* (*Argentina, Squandered Country*), edited by Aguilar, 2003. The article's principal argument is the one developed here.

14. Interview with sociologist Martin Schorr, www.lavaca.org.

15. This study also points out which companies carried out the most layoffs in the 1995–1999 quinquennium. The Spanish Telefónica and French Telecom phone companies headed the list. The electric companies Edesur and Edenor, the railway company Metrovías and, of course, the oil company Repsol-YPF (which cut almost a third of its personnel in those five years) followed. These companies were the benefactors of the privatization of Argentina's public resources and services.

16. The *cacerolazos*, or pot-banging protests, played a central role in the Argentinazo revolt that caused de la Rúa's resignation. A survey conducted by the consultancy firm Hugo Haime y Asociados that interviewed 400 people in the Federal Capitol and Greater Buenos Aires registered the following: "One in three inhabitants of the Federal Capitol and Greater Buenos Aires participated in the *cacerolazos* or neighborhood assemblies. It is a very high ratio. Concretely, it means that 2.5 million people participated or participate in the protests, most of them banging pots on their balconies or doorsteps," in *Pagina/12*, March 10, 2002.

17. Equis Consultancy Firm, June 2004 report, based on INDEC (National Statistics and Census Institute) statistics. *Clarín*, June 28, 2004.

18. Naishtat, Silvia and Pablo Maas, *El Cazador* (*The Hunter*) (Buenos Aires: Editorial Planeta, 2000).

19. Alfredo Yabrán, postal boss suspected of involvement in dirty businesses; implicated in the 1997 assassination of photojournalist José Luis Cabezas. His end was just as obscure. He committed suicide in 1998 while a fugitive from justice. A few weeks earlier he had said "power is impunity" in an interview with *Clarín*.

20. Naishtat and Maas, *El Cazador*.

21. *Alfajores* are Argentine pastries. They are small, round, soft cakes, usually with caramel filling and chocolate covering.

22. Bauman, Zygmunt, *Liquid Modernity* (Cambridge: Polity Press, 2000). The quotation is indirect, translated back into English from the Spanish translation.

23. Intervention of Representative Gustavo Eduardo Gutiérrez of the Democratic Party of Mendoza. Ordinary session of the House of Representatives on May 23, 2002.

24. Bauman, *Society Under Siege*.

25. Méda, Dominique, *El trabajo* (*Work*) (Paris: Gedisa, 1998).

26. Engels, Frederich, Introduction to Karl Marx' *Wage Labor and Capital*, http://www.marxists.org/archive/marx/works/1847/wage-labour/intro.htm/.

27. Lavaca.org is organized as a worker cooperative.

28. Bauman, *Society Under Siege*.

Chapter One: Zanón

1. Luis "Gordo" Valor was the infamous leader of a gang of bank and armored car robbers. The Buenos Aires police force was deeply involved in Valor's gang and many of the robberies.

2. Many of the kidnappings during the military dictatorship that resulted in 30,000 disappearances were carried out in then infamous green Ford Falcons. Threatening phone calls, usually advising the victim to leave the country, were also a hallmark of the dictatorship.

3. Argentina's principal daily newspaper.

4. A green tea from northern Argentina and Paraguay, customarily drunk at all times of day and night throughout Argentina, Paraguay, and Uruguay. It is usually drunk out of a dried pumpkin or wooden container with a metal filtered straw.

5. Domingo Cavallo was economy minister under Menem and again during de la Rúa's last term until being ousted by the popular rebellion of December 2001. Amalita Fortabat is a concrete conglomerate owner. Franco Macri is a pro-Menem businessman and politician. His son Mauricio is the owner of the Boca Juniors soccer club and a possible right-wing candidate for the 2007 presidential elections.

6. Organizations of the unemployed, known for their tactics of blocking roads.

7. A charity fund for children.

8. Thin, breaded meat filets.

Chapter Two: Brukman

1. Elite police force.

2. Highway that marks the limit between the city that is the federal capital and the greater metropolitan area of Buenos Aires.

3. Aníbal Ibarra, then-city mayor.

4. After the expulsion on April 18, 2003, the workers pitched a tent on the plaza on Jujuy and México Avenues, fifty meters from the factory. They protested there until October of 2003, when they won the expropriation of the factory.

5. She is referring to Cecilia Martínez, who ran in the Buenos Aires legislative elections on the Socialist Workers Party (PTS) ticket.

6. José Roselli, House Representative of the Self-Determination and Liberty Party.

7. She is referring to the handkerchiefs with a smile printed on them, to be used at protests to fight the effects of tear gas. The Brukman workers sewed them with borrowed sewing machines.

8. An important avenue of downtown Buenos Aires, where the Congress is located, about twelve blocks from Plaza de Mayo and the Presidential Palace, where the protests had begun and were being dispersed.

9. The Justicialist Party.

10. Antonio Cafiero, the old leader of the Justicialist Party. He was Governor of the Province of Buenos Aires (1987–1991), House Representative (1985), and later Senator.

11. Organization of unemployed workers tied to the Workers' Party.

12. National Institute of Associations and Social Economy, where worker cooperatives have to register.

13. Eduardo Murúa, leader of the National Movement of Reclaimed Companies (MNER) and member of the IMPA worker cooperative.

14. University group of the PTS.

15. Work Plan, a subsidy for the unemployed.

16. Center of Professionals for Human Rights.

17. The factory obtained the definitive expropriation on November 25, 2004, one month after this interview.

18. Leader of the Madres de Plaza de Mayo, organization of the mothers of those disappeared by the dictatorship.

19. University student organization.

20. Wife of Eduardo Duhalde, vice president in the Carlos Menem administration, 1989–1995, and provisional president in 2002–2003.

21. Alternative media organizations linked to the PTS. They have produced various documentaries about the Brukman struggle.

Chapter Three: Crometal

1. *Corralito*, or little pen, was the name given to the measure implemented by de la Rúa's government in late 2001 that froze Argentines' savings. This was the immediate cause of the cacerolazos carried out in front of many banks across the country.

2. A small Argentinian socialist group.

Chapter Four: Chilavert

1. CGTA: Dissident labor union federation that opposed the main CGT's pact with the

dictatorship of Juan Carlos Onganía (1966–1970). Established in 1868, it was dissolved by 1972 due to the arrest of most of its leaders.

2. Founder of the CGTA and Graphic Union leader. Exiled during the military dictatorship in 1976, he returned to Argentina and the head of the Graphic Union, which he led throught the mid-1980s.

3. 1845 naval battle against an Anglo-French fleet.

4. José Luis Chilavert: Paraguayan soccer goalie and star of the Argentine team, Vélez Sarsfield, on which he played.

5. The colloquial name of the La Matanzas River that forms the southern border of the Buenos Aires federal district.

6. A play on words in Spanish. *Naturaleza muerta* (literally dead nature), in art, means "still life." Here, the bricked-up hole above the the still life is referred to as *naturaleza viva*, or "living nature."

Chapter Five: Sime

1. *Huevos*, in Spanish, also refers to "balls" (testicles).

2. Native American tribe from northeastern Argentina and Paraguay.

Chapter Six: Conforti

1. QUEREMOS TRABAJAR, in Spanish.

2. Informal name for the economic measures taken by the Argentine government in December 2001, effectively freezing most bank accounts.

Chapter Seven: Renacer

1. Construction worker from the Continental factory of Ushuaia, killed by police at a demonstration against the brutal ejection of that factory's workers on April 12, 1995.

2. Analogous to a union executive council in the United States.

3. Central de Trabajadores Argentinos: progressive trade union federation founded in 1992. It has just over a million members, mainly from the public sector.

4. Organization of unemployed workers.

Chapter Eight: IMECC

1. The CGT, the General Confederation of Workers, is the mainstream Peronist union federation. The CTA, the Argentine Workers Center, is a dissident union federation

founded in 1991. It tends to organize public sector workers and has a more liberal social and political profile than the CGT.

2. In March of 2004 Kirchner turned the former Navy Mechanical School (ESMA) into a
    museum dedicated to the memories of the 30,000 people disappeared by the military
    dictatorship. Many human rights organizations participated in organizing the Museo
    de la Memoria Nunca Más ("Never Again" Memorial Museum).

3. Teresa Rodríguez and Anibal Verón were unemployed workers and piquetero activists.
    They are memorialized in the names of two of the leading militant piquetero organiza-
    tions, the Movimiento Teresa Rodríguez (Teresa Rodríguez Movement) and the Anibal
    Verón Movimiento de Trabajadores Desocupados (Anibal Verón Unemployed Workers
    Movement).

4. In Spanish, the chants are "IMECC es de los trabajadores, y al que no le gusta, se jode,
    se jode" and "Qué te pasa che milico / qué amargado se te ve / no te pagan un carajo /
    pero igual los defendés."

5. A government program providing microcredit to encourage self-employment.

6. In Spanish the chants are "Y ya lo ve, hoy les ganamos otra vez," "Qué boludos, ahora
    el desalojo se lo meten en el culo," and "Mirá, mirá, sacale una foto, se vuelen a la 11ª
    con el culo roto."

Chapter Ten: Comercio y Justicia

1. Córdoba's nickname, referring to its history of higher education. Jesuits founded Latin
    America's second university in Córdoba in 1614.

2. During the economic crisis in 2001, Argentine banks didn't allow the citizens to with-
    draw their own money from the bank.

3. In Spanish, refered to as *huevos*.

4. Media Investment Company: formed by Argentina's two largest media conglomerates,
    the Clarín Group and the Nación Group, and the Spanish Correo Group.

5. A joint government-private fund that provides credit to small businesses.

6. An economic think-tank launched by thirty-four businesses in Córdoba in 1977.

7. Organization of sons and daughters of those disappeared during Argentina's military
    dictatorship.

Chapter Eleven: The Movements

1. In Spanish, "Unidad de los trabajadores. Y al que no le gusta, se jode."

2. Social economy: the sector of the economy that includes nonprofit and voluntary and
    community-based enterprises.

3. Carlos Gardel is the most famous Argentine tango singer of all time.

4. Colonel Aldo Rico led an uprising against Raúl Alfonsin's government in 1987 to demand an end to trials against military officials for crimes during the dictatorship. He was later elected to Congress and became mayor of San Miguel in Greater Buenos Aires.

5. Journalist and deputy of the Officialist Party for the Democratic Revolution.

6. Montoneros was a youth organization of the revolutionary left sector of Peronism officially constituted in 1970. Yet, after returning from exile in 1973 and assuming his third term as president, Perón sided with the right-wing sector of his broad movement. Montoneros became a clandestine organization on May 1, 1974, and was persecuted by the government's paramilitary Argentine Anticommunist Alliance. It was eventually wiped out by the military dictatorship that took power in 1976.

Publisher's Acknowledgments

Haymarket Books wishes to thank the many people who collaborated on this project. First and foremost are the compañeros from lavaca, principally its founding members: Claudia Acuña, Diego Rosemberg, and Sergio Ciancaglini. Without the thoughtful and patient efforts of Lance Selfa, we could not have published this book. With the very hard work of Katherine Kohlstedt, Federico Moreno, Julian Massaldi-fuchs, Avi Lewis, and Lance Selfa, we have a wonderful translation from the original Spanish. And most importantly, of course, to the many thousands of workers in the reclaimed factories who inspire us and have given us a glimpse of what a world "without bosses" could look like.

About the Authors

The **lavaca collective** is a worker-run cooperative of journalists dedicated to chronicling the Argentine social movements that arose with the 2001 Argentinazo. Sin Patrón, originally published in 2004, was lavaca's first book. To find out more about lavaca and its publications, visit lavaca's Web site at www.lavaca.org.

Avi Lewis is one of Canada's most controversial and eloquent media personalities. His first feature documentary with Naomi Klein, *The Take*, follows Argentina's new movement of worker-run businesses. In the late 1990s, as the host and producer of *counterSpin* on CBC Newsworld, he presided over more than 500 nationally televised debates in three years. His recent television series, *The Big Picture with Avi Lewis*, combined hard-hitting documentaries and town hall debates.

Naomi Klein is the award-winning author of the international bestseller, *No Logo: Taking Aim at the Brand Bullies*, which has been translated into 28 languages and has over a million copies in print. She writes an internationally syndicated column for the *Nation* magazine and the *Guardian* newspaper. Her articles have appeared in *Harper's*, the *Globe and Mail*, and the *New York Times*. Her forthcoming book *The Shock Doctrine: The Rise of Disaster Capitalism* will be published in 2007. More information can be found at www.nologo.org.

Also from Haymarket Books

The Communist Manifesto: A Road Map to History's Most Important Political Document

Karl Marx and Frederick Engels, edited by Phil Gasper • Includes the full text of the Manifesto, with commentaries, annotations, and additional works by Marx and Engels. ISBN 1931859256.

No One Is Illegal: Fighting Racism and State Violence on the U.S./Mexico Border

Justin Akers Chacón and Mike Davis • *No One Is Illegal* debunks the leading ideas behind the often violent right-wing backlash against immigrants.

The Dispossessed: Chronicles of the *Desterrados* of Colombia

Alfredo Molano • Here in their own words are the stories of the Desterrados, or "dispossessed"—the thousands of Colombians displaced by years of war and state-backed terrorism, funded in part through U.S. aid to the Colombian government. With a preface by Aviva Chomsky.

Subterranean Fire: A History of Working-Class Radicalism in the United States

Sharon Smith • Subterranean Fire brings working-class history to light and reveals its lessons for today. ISBN 193185923X

Vive la Revolution: A Stand-up History of the French Revolution

Mark Steel • An actually interesting, unapologetically sympathetic and extremely funny history of the French Revolution. ISBN 193185937X.

Soldiers in Revolt: GI Resistance During the Vietnam War

David Cortright with a new introduction by Howard Zinn • "An exhaustive account of rebellion in all the armed forces, not only in Vietnam but throughout the world."—New York Review of Books ISBN 1931859272

About Haymarket Books

Haymarket Books is a nonprofit, progressive book distributor and publisher, a project of the Center for Economic Research and Social Change. We believe that activists need to take ideas, history, and politics into the many struggles for social justice today. Learning the lessons of past victories, as well as defeats, can arm a new generation of fighters for a better world. As Karl Marx said, "The philosophers have merely interpreted the world; the point however is to change it."

We take inspiration and courage from our namesakes, the Haymarket Martyrs, who gave their lives fighting for a better world. Their 1886 struggle for the eight-hour day, which gave us May Day, the international workers' holiday, reminds workers around the world that ordinary people can organize and struggle for their own liberation. These struggles continue today across the globe—struggles against oppression, exploitation, hunger, and poverty.

It was August Spies, one of the Martyrs who was targeted for being an immigrant and an anarchist, who predicted the battles being fought to this day. "If you think that by hanging us you can stamp out the labor movement," Spies told the judge, "then hang us. Here you will tread upon a spark, but here, and there, and behind you, and in front of you, and everywhere, the flames will blaze up. It is a subterranean fire. You cannot put it out. The ground is on fire upon which you stand."

We could not suceed in our publishing efforts without the generous financial support of our readers. Many people contribute to our project through the Haymarket Sustainers program, where donors receive free books in return for their monetary support. If you would like to be a part of this program, please contact us at info@haymarketbooks.org.